The Witch's Survival Guide

Also by Jennifer Lane:

The Wheel: A Witch's Path to Healing Through Nature (2021)

The Black Air (autumn 2023)

The Witch's Survival Guide

Spells for Healing from Stress and Burnout

Jennifer Lane

1 3 5 7 9 10 8 6 4 2

First published in 2023 by September Publishing

Copyright © Jennifer Lane 2023

Typeset by Ed Pickford

Printed in Denmark on paper from responsibly managed,
sustainable sources by Nørhaven

ISBN 9781914613340
Ebook ISBN 9781914613357

September Publishing
www.septemberpublishing.org

To all my fellow witches who
feel at home in nature

Author's note

This book is not intended to replace medical advice but can be used alongside it to complement and enhance the healing journey.

How to use this book

If you are new to rituals and spells then I suggest you work carefully through Part 1 before moving on to Part 2 in order to get comfortable with common aspects of a witchcraft practice. If you are already well versed in the ways of magick, then by all means dive straight in to Part 2 and dip in and out of Part 1 as your fancy takes you.

Contents

Opening

The sun is shining and I am sitting in a hedgerow.

We are in the midst of a heatwave; I watch the long, shining grasses in the fields as they catch the sun's rays like blades of gold. My daily walk consists of a loop past tumbledown ivy-strewn cottages, through cow fields and then over the canal and back around. I am allowing myself an extra-long lunch break, giving me plenty of time for a saunter in the sun.

The hill rises in front of me as I walk past hawthorn trees that had only a few months before been almost entirely white. Now they are hazes of green. Inside their branches, I hear the peeps and questioning pips of a robin, its ragged-looking breast about to shed its summer plumage. I turn the corner onto a cobbled lane bordered by hedgerows. On my left is an incredible tangled mass of brambles, nettles and more hawthorn, and on my right an abundance of ripening pink rosehips. I smile at the jumbled disorder of plants. The modern mind has been arranged by society to keep our roads and gardens razor-tidy to within an inch of their life (quite literally); disorder and unconformity can sometimes set people on edge. But not here in the countryside. These hedgerows might appear unkempt to others but so many creatures depend on this messiness. Right now, the hedgerows are buzzing and quivering, humming and alive. Bees, ladybirds, shrews, sparrows and caterpillars all watch, confer and wait around me. A baby blackbird scuffles out of the brambles as if sharply shoved by the roots below it. It is still white around the mouth, a sign of a new fledgling. I give it a wide berth and a respectful nod as I pass slowly. It doesn't jerk away back into the foliage, only bobs its knees like a dipper as if returning my nod.

An alcove in the hedge makes a convenient sitting spot – so long as I don't move much and risk making an enemy of the dog rose bushes around me.

I realise then how encompassed I am by the four elements – Earth, Air, Fire and Water. Above me, the sun is blazing, leaving no doubt over its fiery nature; the air is filled with the sounds of birdsong and the occasional swell of crickets. Directly behind me in the full shade of trees is a small lake inhabited by minnows, sturgeons, coots and a lone heron. And how could I forget the earth? The flowers around me, the ground below my feet – the earth element is blooming everywhere at this time of year.

I sit for a while storing this memory up for winter like I am gathering fresh fruit to survive the darker days.

✦

As a green witch, the spring and summer months are by far my favourite of the year. While I might come across as calm and maybe sometimes even aloof, inside I'm squealing like a giddy child when I see the first celandine of spring. Those happy yellow faces along the pathway make me hop around in glee.

But why do spring and summer excite me so much? Surely witches were born for long autumn nights with leaves riffling about their ankles?

When the first notes of September's crispness crinkle the morning air, my body starts to recoil. This means that the darker months are coming. For many, autumn means pumpkins, rainy afternoons curled up with a book and – of course – Halloween. But my favourite Pagan festival isn't Halloween (or Samhain as it is known in the witching world), it is the beautiful May Day festival of Beltane held under budding sunshine; I sometimes wish there was a world I could exist in where I was perpetually surrounded by the white fuzz of spring blossom.

I have had seasonal affective disorder (SAD) for as long as I can remember. When the daylight begins to fade at 3.00 p.m., so does my energy and, with it, my happiness. According to the Royal College of Psychiatrists, approximately three people in every hundred have SAD[1] but, in my experience speaking to friends, family members and colleagues each winter, I think that this number is much higher. It's something I had always tried to control but had been predominantly unsuccessful – until I rediscovered my witchcraft practice.

When writing my book *The Wheel: A Witch's Path to Healing Through Nature*, I put witchcraft to the test. I was chronically exhausted and constantly breaking down in a pre-pandemic world from burnout, which has been defined as mental exhaustion from continuous effort. I felt trapped in a toxic workplace environment that had motivational slogans on its walls but senior management who shattered coffee mugs against the wall if they didn't get their way. I felt so lost. How had I ended up at this place? How could I get out? But it wasn't just this specific workplace; it was office culture as a whole – something I had struggled with since I got my first job at age twenty-two. And to make things worse, as soon as autumn and winter hit, I felt practically useless. I was existing in fight-or-flight mode and struggling with the strange physical and mental symptoms of anxiety and deep depression.

What I experienced is scarily common. The modern world has pushed so many of us to breaking point. Edged us away from the world's seasonal cycles until our minds almost forget them. But our bodies cannot.

Humans were not designed for constant notifications, emails, meetings and commuting. We were meant for a very different life – one that connects us with swaying trees, wild creatures and the rush of the elements across our skin. We were meant to feel the magick of being at one with nature.

However, the patterns of our lives have become unrecognisable from what they would have once been even 200 years ago. Stress has been said to occur when 'aspects of the environment overwhelm people. That is, people feel stressed when too much is expected of them, or when events seem scary or worrisome.'[2] In the short period that technology has revolutionised the world, our bodies have not been able to keep up with the new fast-paced lifestyles forced upon us, leaving many people with burnout, feeling frantic and out of control. While stress has always been a factor in human lives, the imposition of targets, long days, blue light and crowded commutes has compacted our stress. The UK's Health and Safety Executive estimated that in 2020/21 there were 822,000 workers affected by work-related stress, depression or anxiety and found that these conditions accounted for 50 per cent of all work-related instances of ill health.[3]

Society gives us neither the time nor resources to cope with stress – and the longer periods of pressure continue, the more likely they are to manifest as long-term trauma in the body. Common side effects of this include feeling overwhelmed, strange physical sensations, having racing thoughts or difficulty concentrating, trouble sleeping, panic, dissociation and avoidance. These symptoms are very similar to those of someone experiencing post-traumatic stress disorder.

But there are things that can help.

In order to heal our minds and bodies from the stress that the world's current structures perpetuate, many studies have recommended living a life in nature and one that is connected to the earth. Being exposed to the rush of running water, the sound of birdsong on the air, the thrum of the sun's pulse and the unshakeable green world around us has the power to reset the mind, body and soul. The elements of Earth, Air, Fire and Water have what it takes to make us well again.

Back in 2018, between fitful moments of sleep and the stress-related pain that rocketed through my knuckles and wrists, I knew I needed to do something to get me back to myself. The nature-loving child I had once been felt like a scuffed school photograph lost at the bottom of a drawer. Who was I now that I had lost my connection to my childhood self?

What if I could return to and reconnect with the green and natural lives my ancestors would have lived? What if I could tap into the deep magick that resides in the plants, trees and ancient places of this world?

What if I could use magick to heal?

I decided to rekindle the love of witchcraft and magick that had got me through my early teens. Back in those days, there had been lazy Sunday afternoons copying out Celtic Ogham into a paperback journal, trance-like meditations on my bedroom floor surrounded by my favourite teddies, and the frequent days lying in my grandparents' garden soaking up the energy of the beech and pear trees that bordered it. Perhaps these things weren't the average pastimes of a thirteen-year-old but, hey, I never professed to be normal.

This connection with nature has always been a big part of my craft. The green, natural world offers us the tools and medicine we need to help us come back to ourselves and shed the anxiety of modern life.

That is why I'm writing this book.

In this book, I want to share some of the knowledge, rituals and spells that have helped me to heal from a world that was not intended for soft, caring or spiritual people. This book gives spells, rituals and elemental magick for those dealing with the stresses and strains of home and the outside world of presentations and deadlines. Through guided spell work, those with a love of green and positive witchcraft can manage stress and anxiety, harnessing the natural forces of the four elements – Earth, Air, Fire and Water – to cure and restore their souls.

Witchcraft brought me back to myself. This book shows you how you too can take back control of your busy life through the healing power of the craft.

Here in the hedgerow, I am reconnecting to the joy of the natural world. The elements cluster around me, touching my skin, waiting to hear what I might ask of them.

Part One

The Witch's Journey to Healing

1

Finding Witchcraft

Discovering the
right path for you

In the last 20-plus years, I have worked with many different forms of witchcraft in search of the one that felt right to me. I've followed complicated rituals that involved layers of initiation, I have worked with different covens, I have danced in the woods and I have spent hours in meditative quiet in front of my own sacred altar. But nothing has felt more like 'me' than the solitary green witch path.

I have learned to never stick with a practice that feels abrasive to you. Wherever your witchcraft journey takes you, always do what resonates with you to your core and what speaks to your soul.

So what does my path as a green witch involve? Basically, you spend a lot of time with your face in wildflowers.

A green witch is someone who celebrates the cycles of Mother Earth, practises Earth magick and who has a love of all things green and growing. My magick comes out best when I use herbs and when I walk barefoot in my garden and let the swirls of soil imprint themselves on my soles.

My main activities as a green witch involve growing and harvesting herbs to use in tinctures, teas, vinegars and oxymels, tuning into the cycles of the moon, getting lost in wild places and giving back to the beings (seen and unseen) of the natural world.

While most witches have a complete adoration for the natural world, we do have another trick up our trailing sleeves. Many witches practise the arts of spellcraft and magick.

Magick

Like many Pagan folk, I tend to use the word magick with a 'k' to differentiate it from what you'd find at a sideshow act led by The Incredible Fandango. Of course, the word 'magic' is completely fine but if you see it spelt with a 'k' then you know why.

But what is magick?

Having explored different perspectives, this is what I have come to believe:

Magick is a spiritual force that can be used to enhance, influence or change the way a future event happens.

What is a Pagan?

'Pagan' is the overarching term for those with a spiritual connection with the land and the four elements. Many folk who follow Paganism believe nature to have a consciousness that can be tapped into through magickal workings. We hold a reciprocal relationship with the 'more-than-human' world, honouring its cycles, leaving it offerings and giving thanks for its abundance. It is a very grounding path, one that celebrates Mother Earth.

There are many ways that a magickal practitioner can do this, such as through a spell, a charm, a ritual, a sigil or a potion. However you choose to harness the power of magick, having a strong intention and focus behind your working is key. The magickal forces need direction and won't listen if your instructions are filled with ifs, buts and maybes. Working magick also involves a strong sense of self, knowing your own will and being aware of the magickal correspondences of the planets, herbs and times of the moon cycle to enhance your power.

Some believe that magick is constantly around us, waiting for us to grasp it and use it. Others say we need to enter another state of consciousness to tap into the energy of the universe and some say we need to speak to gods and goddesses in order to ask their permission. I believe in a combination of all three. But whatever you believe, magick is a special power that needs to be handled with respect, care and love. If used unwisely, it may bring about unexpected and negative repercussions.

Something that's important to note is that you may often come across spells, rituals and other magickal practices that involve many different tools or ingredients. While these things are nice to have, true witchcraft needs very little, except:

✦ **yourself**

✦ **a connection to nature**

✦ a direct intention (see chapter 4 for more on declaring your intention).

Your magick does not need fancy, expensive tools, crystals or rare herbs in order to succeed, no matter how much people try and push their goods your way. Tools may enhance your work but, if you don't have a particular ingredient or item, there will always be a substitute. For crystals, clear quartz can represent any other crystal as it has a pure energy. In candle magick, a white candle can replace any other colour. Many items can be sourced from nature, such as a sturdy twig or branch to use as a wand, or a beautiful stone to represent the element of Earth. If you do not possess a cauldron, a kitchen bowl or pan works in exactly the same way. One thing to remember is that if you are using everyday items from your kitchen or living space, always cleanse them first (see sage cleansing on page 47) to remove any stagnant or negative energies that have accumulated in them over time. Cleansing an object makes it ready for magickal use. Never feel pressured to buy anything that does not sit comfortably with you or is out of your price range just because you feel you need it to be a witch. You are a witch in and of yourself.

Wicca

Throughout this book, you'll find an array of green witchery but you'll also come across an eclectic mix of practices, primarily from the Wiccan tradition as Wicca is where I first started my witching path and I continue to use its teachings in much of my current practice. Wicca is a form of positive, ceremonial magick that believes in a goddess and a god and celebrates eight seasonal festivals – such as the spring equinox and the summer solstice – depicted on the Wheel of the Year (see glossary) to promote a deep connection with nature.

I always try to follow two of the tenets of Wicca that resonate with me in my practice, but they are also good ways to go about your daily life. The first tenet speaks of the:

Threefold Law: whatever we put out into the universe, we receive back to us times three.

So if we decide to hex our ex and make sure they get demoted from their job, your own company might announce redundancies in a few months' time with you in the firing line. What goes around comes around – call it karma or whatever resonates with you. However, if we ask the universe to help us grow our self-confidence after the break-up, we will begin to find ourselves meeting new, better-suited people who are attracted to our newfound sense of self. Sending out positive energy into the world will only reap more benefits in the long run.

The other tenet I stand by is something we would all do good to live by:

'And it harm none, do as ye will.'

2

Discovering the elements

The elements have always been the strongest way for me to connect with my witchcraft practice: they are all around us all the time, a constant reminder of our relationship with the world.

Little me, on discovering aged eight that my Aries star sign was ruled by Fire, immediately felt powerful. I wasn't the typical cardinal fire-sign child – my voice didn't carry further than 20cm and I wasn't sporty or energetic like all the astrology charts said I would be – but fire fascinated me. As a teen, I found myself so attracted to candles and could get lost in the movement of the fluid flame. I would sneak the kitchen matchbox up to my room under my pyjamas so I could meditate and scry using candles, the outline leaving a glowing white impression etched into my eyelids when I closed my eyes.

Fire was my first elemental love. But as my witchcraft practice grew, so did my love of all the elements – they are our deep connectors to nature.

The Four Classical Elements – Earth, Air, Fire and Water – were said to be the four constituents of everything in our world. In a pre-scientific time without access to microscopes, almost all early cultures wanted to discover what the world was made up of – the essences of heaven and earth. While the concept of the elements can be found across Babylonia, Persia, Japan, China and India, it was the Ancient Greeks that solidified our idea of the Four Classical Elements in around 450 BCE. For a long time, people argued about which was the most important element and whether we needed more of a specific one to survive, but the philosopher Empedocles (*c.* 490–*c.* 430 BCE) believed that each was just as important as the others and that they were all linked together in a cosmic way. The writer and philosopher Aristotle (384–322 BCE) believed that Earth, Air, Fire and Water were the four building blocks needed for life to exist and really cemented the idea of the elements in our consciousness. Each of the elements was seen as having a direct relationship with one another: so, while the masculine element of Fire existed above us (in the form of sunlight), the feminine Water element existed below us (in the form of lakes, rivers and the sea but also moisture in the earth). The feminine element of Earth was below our feet, supporting us, while masculine Air existed around and above us. Elements were attributed a gender based on traditional ideas of femininity and masculinity, with Fire and Air viewed as active, swirling forces while Earth and Water were seen as serene and calming powers. Here in the twenty-first century, we might wish to throw these labels out the window and see these traits as universal qualities, but you will still often see these terms used throughout different magickal practices so this is something to be aware of and to challenge. The Greeks thought that if the four elements ruled everything in the universe, then surely they would rule our bodies and our personalities too. It was in this period that each of the elements became associated with different traits and body parts, an idea that persisted until modern times.

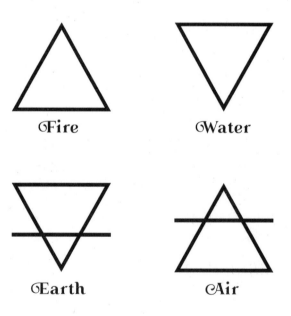

Fire   Water

Earth   Air

What do the elements broadly rule over?

Earth	Air	Fire	Water
Stability	Inspiration	Passion	Emotion
Nurture	Communication	Creativity	Intuition
Nourishment	Clarity	Vitality	Softness

Note: *While this book explores the four elements, I want to acknowledge that this perspective is a very Western one. In Eastern traditions, some elemental correspondences may differ and the Five Element theory – which says there are five elements: Fire, Earth, Metal, Water and Wood – has been used in practices like Traditional Chinese Medicine since the fifth century. If you'd like to find out about other kinds of elemental practices, I've put a list of resources at the back of this book.*

The four elements correspond to modern ideas about matter: solid/Earth, liquid/Water, gas/Air and plasma/ Fire, but there was also believed to be a fifth element – a spiritual one that made up the stars and heavenly, spiritual realms. Aristotle named this fifth element Aether. Nowadays, witches and Pagan folk often debate the nature of 'Aether', with some believing it is the substance that other dimensions and spiritual planes are made of, and others preferring to see it as the fabric of magick itself. For me, I believe aether to be connected to the spirit world, but it is not an 'element' we'll be focussing on too closely in this book.

The herbalist Nicholas Culpeper (1616–1654), famous for *The English Physician* (also known as *Culpeper's Complete Herbal*), integrated ideas of astrology and the elements into his work. Among the work of other notable Early Modern herbalists, his writing is still a strong base for anyone practising herb lore and healing today. Culpeper drew heavily from medieval texts that incorporated Ancient Greek knowledge and based his ideas on the theory of the four humours, which were ruled over by the Four Classical Elements. Taking from these ideas, Culpeper says, 'for in truth, nothing is simple but pure elements; all things else are compounded of them'. Each area of the body was given a ruling element and every herb was given a corresponding element. For example, the common lavender is ruled over by the planet Mercury – the planet of communication – making it an Air herb. In turn, this airy link makes lavender a good herb to use to heal the respiratory system and asthma.

Witchcraft, as a spiritual path that works so closely linked with nature, enveloped the elements into the practice with ease. Working with the elements has been passed down through the centuries and is now one of the most central parts of a general witchcraft practice. You likely know the element your zodiac sign is ruled by or you may already have an element that calls to you. Perhaps you feel most at ease by the sea or maybe you love to feel invigorated by a blast of country air. They are things to be revered – they are the building blocks of all life, after all – and also have a consciousness that can be tapped into like a font of knowledge and advice.

The elements are always near us, brushing our skin with their presence. Even in the greyest office block, we can feel the strong foundations of the building stretching into the Earth and the light of the sun coming through the blinds. They are always there for us to work with – if only we know how to reach out to them.

Bringing the elements into magickal workings

So, how do you work together with the elements in your witchcraft practice and how can you harness their powers for healing?

Understanding

AS WITH ANY relationship, it begins with understanding. Spend time in nature and get to know how each element feels on your skin and in your bones; close your eyes and spread your toes on the Earth, expose the skin of your neck to feel the Air play against the softest parts of you. At the same time, you can deepen your knowledge of each element by getting to know its correspondences.

The elements can help to alleviate:

burnout

✦

stress

✦

anxiety

✦

overwhelm

✦

depression

✦

panic attacks

✦

dissociation

✦

procrastination

✦

self-sabotage

For example, if you find yourself feeling low, uncreative and stuck, then the element of Fire will be able to help you blast those emotions away. In Part 2, I'll discuss elemental correspondences and associations; their favourite days of the week, colours and herbs. This knowledge will help to bring you within touching distance of each element.

Communication

THE NEXT STEP is to communicate. Speak to the element and get to know the way it reciprocates. When you welcome the element of Air into your space, you may be met with a sudden gust of wind coming through a window you didn't even know was open. You can speak directly to the element, for example, 'Air, I would love to work with you today and welcome you into this sacred space.'

Once you have engaged the elements and got their attention, they will need direction so that they know how to help you. This can be done through many means, such as through a ritual or spell, which we will go into in the next chapter.

You can also engage with an element by honouring them on your altar (see page 43) so that they are aware you are seeking a connection with them and are giving the right amount of respect.

When you have finished interacting with an element, always remember to thank it and remind it that it is now free to leave your sacred space. Elements also need to go about their day. If they linger too long they can become … difficult.

Earth, Air, Wind and Fire can sometimes be tempestuous, especially when they are not spoken to with respect. Just as Water can provide a soothing dip after a long day, it can also destroy cliff faces and knock boats leagues off their course. Fire can keep you warm and snug on a cold winter's night but can cause unfathomable damage. The elements command a lot of power and use it at their will: politeness and sincere reverence go a long way when asking for help from them. On this point, it's important to note that we never 'use' the elements, we *work with* them. The elements are their own natural forces, not playthings to be toyed with or picked up then cast aside without a care.

Something I have found, however, is that the elements tend to be very sympathetic. I have always treated them kindly and softly and they have treated me the same in return. Perhaps, having been around since the dawn of time, they know the amount of suffering that has existed in this world and want to lend a hand to help restore balance. They have never turned me away except to tell me I am working with the wrong element – if I tune in, they will let me know which one is best to work with in order to get the best result. They can be attentive, willing and perfectly suited companions on your journey back to yourself.

Yes, there is a lot of power behind the elements, but when used as a force of good and healing, and when spoken to with care they will make sure that positivity comes your way.

3

An introduction to rituals and spells

Over the course of this book, we'll be looking at different forms of magickal practice. We can observe the seasons and give thanks to the elements in our everyday lives without involving any magick whatsoever, for example by meditating, cleansing a space or by having a candlelit bath and watching the flames play over the water. However, there are many times when we may wish to harness the powers of magick to change the course of events and bring about a positive outcome.

To achieve the most powerful result, it is important to perform magick with the following three things in mind: intent, desire and drive. If you are carrying out magick just for the fun of it or you just want to see what happens then it is highly unlikely your magick will be successful.

Intent: You have to have a good reason for performing a piece of magick and have thought about your intent inside and out. Ask yourself why you are performing this magick and exactly what you want the outcome to be. Write this down to crystallise the intent in your mind's eye.

Desire: There may be a completely logical reason behind your magick: you have an important day coming up so you want a good night's sleep beforehand – a completely rational thought. But if you're dreading the big day and are looking for an excuse to back out, your sleeping spell won't work, no matter how accurate it is. You need to really want the spell to work.

Drive: The outcome must motivate you. It's not enough to just want the spell to work – the outcome you desire must fill you with passion. You have to want to do everything in your power to get the outcome you need. You need to be willing to put in the legwork and nudge the spell in the right direction, thinking about the outcome every day until it manifests into being.

But how can we work out what form of magick is best for our purposes?

Rituals

A ritual is a ceremony where we honour and observe a particular festival, season, deity or element. The intent behind a ritual is to connect with the world's divine energy and ask for its assistance. For example, on a full moon, we might perform a banishing ritual, asking the moon and the Water element to help us let go of anything holding us back. With the aid of a spiritual being, our outcome is likely to be filled with a high amount of power.

Spells

Think of a spell as a short blast of magick infused with intention. Spells are usually quicker to perform and can be focussed on words or objects. Their power can be enhanced by using corresponding plants, crystals or colours. Creating a charm, amulet or talisman is a form of spell that imbues an object with a specific power when you keep it close.

✦

Both forms of magick are important within witchcraft although it's important to strike a balance. If we are only performing spell work and not finding the time to meditatively connect with the divine, then we might wish to look at why this is. Reflection, meditation and giving gratitude are all equally important and valid parts of a rounded witchcraft practice.

The elements will add potency to both spells and rituals, as will knowing the corresponding moon phases and days of the week on which rituals will be at their most powerful. However, before working a ritual, it is important to work safely by creating a sacred space.

The foundations of ritual work

Casting a circle

No ritual would be complete without a sacred space to perform it in. This is usually in the form of a circle. There are many reasons why we 'cast a circle' before carrying out our ritual work.

1. To contain our magickal workings and focus their power.

2. To keep out any negative energies or spirits that might wish to intrude.

3. To provide a mental and spiritual barrier to the world and create a space where we feel safe to embrace our identity.

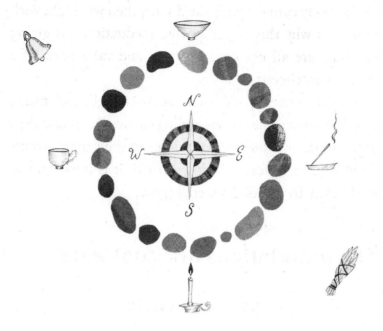

Casting a circle can be done by physically drawing a circle on the ground or through visualisation, but creating one needs time, space and dedication, so be sure to honour this practice and give it the beautiful energy it deserves. A circle is needed when practising ritual work as you are usually working with the elements and quite possibly powerful deities. It is not a requirement for spell work although I often use one for this as well to enhance my workings.

Below is my own method of casting a circle. Other practitioners may do this slightly differently but, in essence, our methods are all the same.

Note: *Living in the northern hemisphere, I start my rituals at the north compass point and move in a clockwise direction. If you practise in the southern hemisphere you may wish to start at the south compass point and move in an anti-clockwise direction.*

You'll need:

+ a space wide enough to stand in and turn around

+ 1 small bowl of earth

+ incense and a holder

+ 1 white candle and holder

+ 1 bowl/cup of water

+ salt

+ sage or a bell for cleansing

+ optional: athame (see page 45)

+ optional: compass.

Note: *When referring to sage throughout this book, I always mean garden or common sage, as opposed to white sage. White sage is a herb sacred to indigenous cultures and is currently being overharvested where it grows naturally on the west coast of North America. Please opt for garden sage in your workings.*

Tip: *When burning sage, always hold a fire-proof bowl or dish below it – I learnt this from singeing the carpet!*

Step One: Getting ready and setting up

1. First of all, find the space where you'd like to create a circle. Make sure you have enough room to stretch out your arms on either side and place additional items.

2. Next, you will need to make sure you know which way you are facing. Take a compass (or observe the sun) and make a note of where north, south, east and west lie.

3. Place your bowl of earth at the north-most point of the space and the incense to the east. Then place the candle in the south and the water to the west.

4. Cleanse the space using your chosen method – either the smoke from a lit bundle of sage, by ringing a bell, or by use of a singing bowl – and allow the smoke or vibrations to move about the space, focussing particularly on your body and any items you'll be using to cast the circle.

5. Before you begin, you might wish to sit in the space for a few moments and breathe in deeply, settling into your practice slowly.

Step Two: Casting the circle

1. Hold out your athame in front of you or, if you don't have one yet, clasp your hands together with your two index fingers outstretched. Beginning at the north, point the athame/your fingers and say: 'With my power, I mark this circle.' Walk in a clockwise direction three times with the athame/your fingers held out, repeating the above words as you go. As you do this, visualise white flames coming from your athame/your fingers and forming a protective barrier around your circle.

2. Take the salt and, starting in the north again, sprinkle this in a clockwise direction, walking three loops of your circle. As you do this, say: 'With this salt, I purify my circle.'

3. Next, we welcome the four elements into the space. This is called 'calling the corners'. The elements bring balance and support to your circle as well their own unique properties. Raise your arms upwards and turn to the north.

4. In a loud, clear voice, say: 'Hail to the powers of the North, by the powers of Earth and stability. I invoke thee, I invoke thee, I invoke thee. Hail and welcome.' As you do this, feel the earth strong below your feet.

5. Turn to the east, light your incense, and with your arms up say, 'Hail to the powers of the East, by the powers of Air and inspiration. I invoke thee, I invoke thee, I invoke thee. Hail and welcome.' Close your eyes and feel the Air element around you – you might experience a sudden breeze or puff of wind as the Air element enters the space.

6. Turn to the south and light your candle. With your arms up, say, 'Hail to the powers of the South, by the powers of Fire and passion. I invoke thee, I invoke thee, I invoke thee. Hail and welcome.' Look out for flickers in your candle or sudden flares of warmth as Fire enters the circle.

7. Lastly, turn to the west and with your arms up say, 'Hail to the powers of the West, by the powers of Water and emotion. I invoke thee, I invoke thee, I invoke thee. Hail and welcome.' Visualise water coming in around your feet. You may feel slightly unstable or as if you are floating.

What are deities?

Deities – gods and goddesses – can form an important part of your magickal practice. Over the millennia, people have called on the services of the gods to enhance their prayers or spellwork. Gods and goddess often have their own specialities – for instance, the Ancient Greek goddess Persephone was the ruler of spring so people would invoke her to ask her for a warm season with the promise of new beginnings. Similarly, the Norse goddess Freya was associated with love and beauty. For those wishing to enhance their own self-love and inner confidence, she might be the one to speak with. These beings exist on a separate magickal plane to ours but we can contact them through ritual work and ask them to help us. Just as when you are working with the elements, deities must be treated with great respect and often require an offering of some kind – such as food, drink or a natural object – as this shows them that you are serious about your request.

Here are some other common deities that you may wish to work with in your practice:

- **Rhiannon** – Celtic goddess of fertility (physical and metaphorical), faeries/Air elementals and ideas coming to fruition
- **Artemis** – Greek goddess of purity, wild animals, nature and the moon
- **Cerridwen** – Welsh goddess of wisdom, shadow work and transformation
- **Venus** – Roman goddess of love and self-love
- **Isis** – Egyptian goddess of healing, magick and protection
- **Hecate** – Greek goddess of magick, witchcraft, the night and crossroads
- **Geb** – Egyptian god of the earth and all things that grow from it
- **Cernunnos** – Celtic god of wild things and places, and fertility.

Many people wish to only work with deities within one pantheon – for example, in the Celtic pantheon or in the Greek – but you may wish to work in a more eclectic way and seek out the gods and goddesses that speak to you personally. Within a ritual, you can speak to a specific deity and bring them into your sacred space to work with you, but most often I welcome in 'the Goddess' – the Greater Mother who is a combination of all the deities in one. She is Mother Earth – she is everything. Choose as you wish and see what fits with your own personal way of working.

Step Three: Welcoming in a deity

1. If you wish to include deities in your practice, now is the time to welcome them into your circle. Some gods and goddesses can be tricky to work with and need a skilled hand or a firm boundary so if deities are not for you or you do not wish to work with any specifically by name, substitute the brackets below for 'universal energy', 'Mother Earth' or, simply, 'the Goddess'.

2. Hold your arms to the sky and say, 'I invoke [name of deity] and welcome them into my circle. Please lend your energies to my magickal workings as I [state the intent of your ritual]. Bless me with your light and your guidance. I invoke thee, I invoke thee, I invoke thee. Hail and welcome.' You may feel a presence enter your circle. Take note of it and maybe even say a few more friendly words to it.

3. Take your athame or your outstretched fingers and point upwards. Say, 'The circle is now cast. As above.' Then touch your athame/fingers to the ground and say, 'So below. So mote it be' (or 'so may it be').

4. You are now ready to perform your ritual.

Tip: *Once you have cast your circle, you won't be able to leave it without breaking the protective barrier. If you need to nip outside the circle for any forgotten items, you will need to begin the circle casting all over again! So be sure you have everything you need for your ritual and spellwork inside the sacred space before you begin.*

Closing a circle

It is important to close a circle after you have finished your work as it releases the elements and chosen deity from the space. If they are forced to linger and stay longer than is necessary they can get mad. They may also stay around your home or in your energy field, which can be confusing for you and rude to them, so make sure to release them once your ritual is complete.

Note: *Closing a circle is performed in an anti-clockwise direction in the northern hemisphere and should be performed in reverse – in a clockwise direction – in the southern hemisphere.*

1. At the end of your ritual, raise your arms into the air and thank the deity or universal energy for their support and guidance. Then say, 'Go now in peace. I un-invoke thee, I un-invoke thee, I un-invoke thee,' feeling their presence leave the circle.

2. Turn to the western point and thank the element of Water for joining you in your circle, then say, 'Go now in peace. I un-invoke thee, I un-invoke thee, I un-invoke thee,' feeling their presence leave the circle.

3. Continue on to the other compass points in an anti-clockwise movement, saying thank you to the elements of Fire, Air and Earth (snuffing out any candles or incense as you go).

4. Once you have reached the northern point, take your athame/pointed fingers and run it/them around the edge of the circle three times in an anti-clockwise motion saying, 'With this athame/my power, the circle is unmade,' as you walk.

5. Visualise the protective light around the circle fading and flowing back into the earth. Hold up your athame or fingers and say, 'As above,' then point to the ground and say, 'So below. So mote it be.'

6. You might feel dizzy after this so remember to ground yourself by kneeling down and placing your hands and forehead on the ground.

Creating an altar

Aside from creating a sacred space within ritual work, you may also wish to dedicate an area to your craft within your home. Many witches like to create a specific space where they can go to practise magick, meditate and connect with themselves. While the natural world is always open to us, a sacred altar in our own homes or gardens that contains our magickal tools can be a more practical place to honour our craft.

An altar is a place of balance and calm, a place where we go to nourish our spirituality.

My own altar is an upturned wooden crate I bought from an outdoor market – so we're not talking anything fancy here! Decorating and consecrating your altar can be a beautiful thing and I know witches with whole rooms dedicated to their altar, ritual tools, offerings and ritual space, but the majority of us do things a bit more simply.

I'll tell you what I have on my Pagan altar so you can see what items resonate with you. There is no set way for your altar to look or the tools it should have on it, but I will run through the more traditional ones and what they symbolise.

A typical altar will contain:

- **an altar cloth.** I have two velvet cloths – a green one to symbolise spring and summer (or Air and Fire) and a purple one to switch things up when autumn and winter (Water and Earth) come around – but you can have just one. These are sometimes stitched with occult symbols or depictions of the moon but mainly they are there on a practical level to protect your space from ash, water droplets or herb spillages.

- **a representation of the Goddess and God.** It's absolutely fine if you do not subscribe to a deity; you can still include a symbol of the divine feminine and masculine that exists within everything. This can be small statues, two Tarot cards, symbols of the Triple Goddess and the Horned God (see below) or the traditional symbols for masculine and feminine.

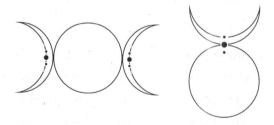

An altar will also hold a witch's ritual tools:

- **an athame.** The athame is a ritual dagger and can be used in spell work to create a boundary, to direct energy or symbolise the divine masculine.

- **a wand.** I have always used a wand and an athame interchangeably. Both are used to store and channel energy.

- **a chalice or cauldron.** Both of these items represent the divine feminine and can be used to contain water, a ritual beverage, or your cauldron can hold the remnants of your spellcraft. They are symbols of abundance and plenty.

- **two candles.** Similar to the representation of the Goddess and God, these two candles signify dark and light, yin and yang – the opposites and balances within our world. You might choose to make one of these candles white and one black, or if that doesn't resonate with you, you can carve different symbols into two candles of the same colour.

- **a pentacle/pentagram.** Many Pagans, Wiccans and witches choose to have a pentacle or a pentagram on their altar. The five points of the pentagram can represent the four elements plus the more mysterious fifth element, aether. The fifth point (usually depicted as the one at the top of the pentagram) can be aether or can sometimes represent the soul or self, putting your own energy among that of the Four Classical Elements.

✦ **an incense holder.** Burning incense represents the eastern point of the compass as well as the element of Air. I also love surrounding myself with this powerful scent during a ritual or in spellwork as I feel it adds another layer of protection to my sacred space.

✦ **a candle snuffer.** While blowing out a candle is fine, this can sometimes mean that we are blowing the potent energies of the candle away from us. By using a candle snuffer (or douter), we are keeping the candle's power close to our chests.

Handy things to have nearby:

✦ extra incense or candles in case you run out unexpectedly

✦ sage for cleansing (by burning)

✦ a robe (OK, this doesn't actually have to live on or nearby your altar but I would strongly advise having a special outfit in which you perform your magickal activities. The day's energies often get stuck in our clothing so being able to get changed into an outfit that is designated for magick is important. I use a long dark pink robe with golden thread in it, which makes me feel confident and powerful.)

✦ matches/a lighter

✦ bowls or candle holders because Pagans need a fire safety course

✦ a boline. This is a sharp, white-handled knife sometimes used for ritual herb preparation or cord cutting ceremonies. Personally, I don't have one (my kitchen knife does a pretty good job) but many witches keep one in their sacred space

✦ ribbons and thread of different colours

✦ your crystal collection.

Cleansing your altar

One of the most important things to do before adding an item to your altar is to cleanse it.

When the spring equinox waves its blossomy hand my way, I take out my green altar cloth and light a twig of dried sage. Sage is known for its cleansing and purifying properties so it is perfect to remove any negative energy that might have gathered in the cloth over the six months it's been locked away. As I allow the sage smoke to move around the altar, I like to say, 'Earth, Fire, Water, Air, cleanse, dismiss, dispel,' at least three times. Visualise the smoke neutralising any energies attached to the object, cutting through anything dark or dense and allowing them to evaporate or sink down into the ground.

Perform this cleansing on the whole of your altar and each of your tools, including crystals and herbs. For more information on smoke cleansing, head to page 110.

✦

Creating sacred space can seem like quite a process if you are new to the craft but it is absolutely vital when you are working with magickal forces, known or unknown. Now you know this important step, you are ready to move on to practising ritual and spellwork.

As you have a good grounding in witchcraft and my particular brand of magick, we'll move on to the main section of this book where we'll do a deep dive into the four elements. In this section, we'll find ways to work together with the elements to create positivity, peace, balance and joy in our lives and to heal from burnout, stress, anxiety and depression.

So, let's take a breath and delve in.

Part 2

Healing with the elements

4

Earth

Grounding, nourishing and resetting

What is your earliest memory of digging in the earth?

Sometimes as a small child, I was let loose in the garden with a trowel and orders to dig holes for new begonias and pansies to live in.

It was my first small taste of wildness. But later in life, I discovered the true power of the earth.

Nature can be a place of mental reprieve and physical shelter from the relentless spin of modern life.

Walking in the woods has always been beneficial for nourishing our bodies, minds and souls – something that indigenous people have long known. The forest was a place to gather berries, kindling, fungi and wisdom. Somewhere to go to meditate, listen, and seek deep knowledge from the interconnected network of the wildwood.

The element of Earth is a deeply nurturing power that connects us with trees, plants, herbs, rocks and the very earth below our feet. It is one of the two feminine elements and has grounding, nourishing and resetting qualities – things that are absolutely vital to us when we are healing. Earth is also linked with the season of winter, a time of year when all in nature is quiet and still, giving us the time to reflect, turn inwards and listen to our intuition. In this respect, I class Earth as an 'introverted element', one that allows us the chance to slip inside ourselves and tune in to our inner wisdom in times of need. Earth may seem like a solid, unyielding force but I personally find it a soft, safe and enveloping space to inhabit.

It is associated with the northern compass point. When I perform my rituals, I always start by facing in a northwards direction, welcoming in the Earth element first to ground me before I start my magickal workings.

When I feel stressed or frazzled, Earth is the first element I turn to for assistance and it is where we will start our elemental journey in this book.

Earth correspondences

Symbol	▽
Direction	North
Zodiac signs	Taurus, Virgo, Capricorn
Alignment	Feminine
Colours	Earthy greens, browns and blacks
Plants	Blackthorn, honeysuckle, mugwort, primrose, patchouli
Crystals	Smoky quartz, tiger's eye, malachite, jet, jasper
Humour	Melancholic (cold and dry)
Moon phases	Waning moon
Elementals	Gnomes, dwarfs, elves, brownies, hobgoblins and leprechauns
Deities	Gaia, Demeter, Rhiannon, Geb, Emesh, Dharā
Tarot	Pentacles
Metals	Iron
Altar representations	Pentacle, items from nature including branches, pine cones, flowers and mounds of earth
Time of day	Dawn
Weekdays	Thursday and Saturday
Heavenly bodies	Venus and Mars
Season	Winter
Opposing element	Air

The significance of trees

Where would we be without trees?

They are our greatest supporters – the oxygen givers, the natural chemists – helping us on a physical, mental and spiritual level, weaving together the health and happiness of humans and wildlife across the planet. We owe them everything we have.

Our society as we know it exists in a hierarchy with human beings at the top, but this idea of humankind as separate in mind and spirit from other species is a relatively new invention. Our ancestors would have lived in a world where trees had spirits, plants helped to heal, and the rocks on the ground held ancient wisdom. In some Native American cultures, trees were called the Standing People, the plants were the Plant People, and the rocks would be the Stone People – all equal to human life.

Our ancestors knew better than anyone the benefits that trees and their deep connection with the Earth element offered us. Many cultures across the world have incorporated a 'tree of life' into their medicine as well as into their spiritual beliefs, from Judaism, Christianity and Islam to Druidry and Buddhism. The vast ancient ash tree, Yggdrasil in Norse culture, linked together the physical and spiritual worlds.

In the Celtic Ogham alphabet, trees hold a lot of symbolism that we can harness in our magickal practices. The birch is a symbol of rebirth. This quality of renewal led to its branches being burned by the Celts to cleanse an area of negative energy: cradles made from birch twigs were said to protect babies with their purifying energy.

We can ask certain trees – the great stewards of the earth – to help us with our healing.

Many of the trees below are symbolic of protection and strength, which are attributes associated with the Earth element. Find a tree whose powers resonate with you and go out into nature to seek its solace.

Trees and their magickal associations

Oak (*Quercus*)

THE OAK IS a sacred tree across many cultures and a Celtic word for 'oak' (Druir) is said to be where the Druids get their name. Indeed, Druids are famed for practising in sacred oak groves.

This tree – the king of the forest – is a symbol of strength (both mental and physical) and wisdom, and can be called upon at times when real resilience is required.

Magickal properties: strength, wisdom, endurance

Ash (*Fraxinus*)

THE WHOLE WORLD was once believed to hang on an ash tree. Both Norse and Celtic cultures saw the ash as central to their mythology, linking us to other spiritual planes. This is perhaps because of ash's incredibly deep roots and tall branches, which stretched to the upper and lower worlds.

In witchcraft, the spirit of the ash tree can be called upon for healing and divination purposes, looking for answers about possible outcomes to a situation.

Magickal properties: healing, divination, life force, creativity

Beech (*Fagus*)

BEECH – THE tree of the writer! This tree has often been linked to time and written wisdom, so channel the beech when you are looking for creative inspiration.

It is a feminine, nurturing tree whose bark brings healing and can be seen as the 'queen' to the oak tree's 'king'. Work with beech when you are looking to reconnect with softness and rest.

Magickal properties: the written word, femininity, learning, understanding, longevity, progress

Rowan (*Sorbus aucuparia*)

YOU'LL KNOW THE rowan tree from its bright red late-summer fruit, which startles the senses on any woodland walk. The rowan is a very protective tree – some sources say it protects ordinary folk from witches if they hang its branches above their door while other sources say witches make their broomsticks out of it.

Call on the rowan in times when you feel you need mental, physical or magickal protection.

Magickal properties: protection, wisdom, courage

Holly (*Ilex*)

THE OAK TREE'S arch nemesis. In folklore, the holly is said to rule over the winter months while the oak is king when the summer comes once more. Holly is another protective tree as its spiky leaves protect its foliage and berries from being stolen – keep a small sprig of holly close to keep negative energies away from you all year round.

Magickal properties: protection from negativity, fertility, life force

Elder (*Sambucus nigra*)

THE 'OLD LADY' of the woods, this friendly witch-crone was said to protect homes from evil spirits. Needless to say, this didn't make her any friends when Christianity took over from the old beliefs and she was viewed negatively for hundreds of years.

Think of elder when you want to protect your sacred space – and drink its berries in tea to fortify yourself with vitamin C in winter.

Magickal properties: protection, death, magick, new beginnings

Hawthorn (*Crataegus monogyna*)

THIS TREE'S WHITE sprays of blossom fill the air with an unusual scent. Known as a faery tree, hawthorn can cause mayhem if you pick its flowers so maybe let them stay put. Perform love and self-love magick under its boughs instead.

Magickal properties: love, self-love, fertility, balance, the otherworld

Blackthorn (*Prunus spinosa*)

VERY SIMILAR TO the hawthorn with its prickly branches and white flowers, the blackthorn creates a blackened skeleton in the winter months. Thanks to its appearance, thorns and dark berries, it is often associated with the underworld and spiritual realms.

Doing some self-reflection and introspection near or under a blackthorn will increase the potency of your work: you may come to some interesting realisations thanks to this otherworldly tree.

Magickal properties: purification, the otherworld, strength, overcoming strife/adversity

Birch (*Betula*)

EVER HEARD OF being 'birched'? Schoolchildren might have once been hit with birch canes to purify the evil out of them. Birch has a long history as a cleansing tool and sitting

below its branches might be just the place to clear your mind and come back to yourself. No self-flagellation involved.

Magickal properties: cleansing/purification, rebirth/new beginnings, spiritual and personal growth

Yew (*Taxus baccata*)

ONE OF THE most sacred trees in the Pagan world, the yew is not only renowned for its fantastic protective abilities but also for its associations with rebirth, death and the otherworld. It is one of the most common trees you will see in Christian graveyards due to its links with immortality – by watching over the headstones, the souls of those who rest beneath them will live forever.

Place your hand on a yew tree when you are in need of otherworldly guidance to point you in the right direction (and always beware of its poisonous berries).

Magickal properties: rebirth, connection to the otherworld/divine, longevity, death (of a situation or a period of time)

Guided meditation for communing with plants and trees for deep healing

Communing with green and living beings such as plants and trees is an important practice. Not only does it allow us to know them better, but by speaking with the guardians of the Earth element we can receive their wisdom and healing.

In my magickal practice, I often allow my own consciousness to reach out to and merge with a tree or a certain plant that I know will bring me aid in a time of need. I do this by visualising my aura expanding and feeling out the consciousness of the being I wish to merge with. This process is a deep form of meditation that allows us to seek healing and create bonds with the natural world.

Let's take the oak tree. Oak trees are traditional symbols of mental and physical strength; a medicine we all welcome from time to time, especially during times of stress or sadness.

The following meditation allows us to join our consciousness with the oak tree when we need to seek its aid. You can also download a recording of this meditation from jenniferlanewrites.com/meditations.

If you wish to perform this exercise quickly or live in an urban area with little access to nature, you don't need to sit with an actual oak tree – you might use a picture of an oak tree or some dried acorns you collected on a walk last year – so long as you connect with the oak and hold it in your mind's eye. However, to really immerse yourself in the practice and to feel its true potency, I would recommend finding a secluded oak tree.

1. *Find a quiet place to sit with your oak tree (or oak tree signifier), breathe deeply, and slip into a meditative state.*

2. *As if you are reaching out your hand, extend your mind to touch the oak's consciousness. Visualise your personal energy lifting from your skin and expanding, feeling out the oak's energy field. How does it feel to you? Is the oak a welcoming or hostile presence? Gently tell the oak your intention of connecting with it for plant medicine, strength and resilience, and ask the tree whether you can work with it today.*

3. *If the answer you feel is yes, then continue with this practice and say thank you. If you feel like the oak's energy is hostile then back away your energy. There could be a multitude of reasons for this; for example, the oak might think you are better placed to work with another tree today. You may have thought you needed to ask for strength but instead you need some deep spiritual cleansing – in this instance, go in search of a local birch tree. Listen to what the oak tells you, thank it, and leave the tree in peace.*

4. *If you are encouraged to continue with this process and you feel comfortable that the oak is ready, use all your senses to scope out the oak. What does it smell like? What does it sound like as the wind touches its leaves? What is its energy like?*

5. *Now you have a feel for the oak tree, begin to merge your mind with it. Find yourself as one with it. What is it like to stand tall and proud as an oak tree? It is time to feel the sun's energy on your face and ask for any medicine that oak wants to bring you. Let this power fill you.*

6. *How do you feel now? Stronger? Taller? More confident? Softly, ease yourself away from the oak and thank it for its healing. Perhaps the oak had a message for you that you want to write down in your journal.*

It may take a few tries to feel a very deep connection but, once you do, this is a skill you can transfer to any plant, stone or tree. If you are looking for psychic protection from toxic people around you, then perhaps the rowan is your go-to tree, or if you require a joyful boost then sunflower energy can help you – a list of plant properties is below. This practice can also be done with crystals and rocks so take a look at the list of crystal correspondences in the appendix on page 212 – whether it's for a physical ailment or an emotional wound – and ask the plant or stone to send you what you need.

Every time you do this, you are not only healing your body and soul, but you are also repairing your connection with the Earth.

A word of caution: Merging with and reaching out to the plant and animal kingdom is usually a very safe practice; however, I would not recommend doing this with humans. People often carry a lot of negative energy in their auric fields, even if they are not aware of it. Steer clear of doing this practice with any person, even if you know them well.

Herbs and plants associated with the Earth element

While all plants, herbs and fungi are 'of the earth', each herb is ruled by a different element. This might seem counterintuitive – how could a plant that grows directly from the soil be anything but 'Earth'? However, plants have myriad qualities that connect them beautifully with the planets, the seasons and the rest of the cosmos. The plants in this section are all overseen by the Earth element, something which often comes across in their 'earthy' or bitter tastes or scents.

Mugwort (*Artemisia vulgaris*)

THE WITCH'S FAVOURITE plant! Mugwort has many associations and has been used for centuries in protection, cleansing and luck magick.

However, mugwort is the cousin of the notorious wormwood plant: drunk in tea, mugwort can induce psychic dreams or visions. While it isn't hallucinogenic, it has been known to make spiritual abilities stronger.

Magickal properties: cleansing, ward against evil, good luck, protection, psychic abilities, intuition

WARNING: Mugwort should not be used by pregnant or lactating women

Honeysuckle (*Lonicera periclymenum*)

THIS CREEPING HEDGEROW plant is associated with prosperity. You might have seen it in country lanes during the summer with its up-curved pink and white petals that look like little horns. Not only does it smell wonderful, but it can help to attract abundance. Use the whole flower or honeysuckle oil in your rituals to invite in more money if financial stresses are contributing to a feeling of overwhelm for you.

As it is ruled by the planet Venus, honeysuckle is also very well-placed in love magick. Using love magick on an unsuspecting person is an ethical no-no, but using it on yourself to inspire self-love is a lovely way to enjoy honeysuckle's effects.

Magickal uses: prosperity, abundance, self-love, friendship, fidelity

Blackthorn (*Prunus spinosa*)

BLACKTHORN FRUIT – the sloe berry – can be used in spellwork, tinctures, jams and, most famously, gin. The deep-purple berry can be dried out and used in protective magick, so if there is someone or something you feel is draining your energy, a charm or pouch of sloes, tourmaline and smoky quartz might suit you well.

Magickal uses: ward against evil, protection, rebirth

Herbal tea and infusions for physical and mental wellbeing

Drinking teas and infusions containing herbs, plants, mushrooms or berries can be an incredibly grounding experience and root us back in our bodies if we are feeling overtaken by outside influences or panic. Coffee and black tea can be overstimulating and can create more problems than they solve, making us anxious, frazzled and filled with adrenaline.

Here are several tea combinations that will help to calm and soothe the body and mind as well as activate the parasympathetic nervous system to lower our heart rates and cortisol levels, offering quick resets in the face of challenging times. Steep these plants in hot water to feel their beautiful benefits.

+ **Anxiety and panic** – chamomile, borage, lemon balm, mint.

+ **Burnout** – oat straw, ashwagandha, birch polypore fungus, holy basil/tulsi, echinacea.

+ **Depression** – rose, nettle, astragalus, ginger, hawthorn berry, cinnamon, blackberry.

+ **Dissociation** – mint, ginger, fennel.

+ **General wellbeing** – green tea, dandelion, turmeric, ginger, mint, elderberry, echinacea.

+ **Insomnia** – chamomile, lavender, valerian.

+ **Overwhelm and stress** – oat straw, rose, raspberry leaf, chamomile, reishi mushroom.

How to prepare herbal tea

1. Place your herbs in a teapot, tea infuser or cafetière and allow them to steep in hot water for 5–10 minutes.

2. Remove the infuser or pour the tea and drink while warm.

3. Imbue your tea with magickal potency: close your eyes and put your hand over the tea, move your hand in a clockwise direction and say the quality you wish the tea to enhance, e.g. 'I am happy' or 'I am calm'. Alternatively, move your hand in an anti-clockwise direction to ask the tea to remove something from your life, e.g. 'Take my anxiety' or 'Take away my stress'.

How to prepare herbal infusions

ALL THE PLANTS listed above contain potent nutrients that will help the body recover. Herbal infusions help to extract the most nutrients. To make an infusion:

1. Half-fill a glass jar or container with your chosen herbs.

2. Fill it with hot water and put the lid on.

3. Allow it to sit for between four and nine hours.

4. Strain the infused water into a cup and drink.

Tip: *Do not use a metal container to create your infusion as some of the metals may seep into the hot water.*

Earth goddesses and gods

Just as there are earthly, physical beings associated with each element (plants, trees and crystals are all 'other-than-human' beings), there are spiritual ones too. Each element is closely linked with a set of deities that reflect its properties. My favourite goddess associated with the element of Earth is the Celtic goddess Rhiannon. A mother goddess who watches over the land and the harvest, she is also a lover of horses and rides through the land on her white horse, one hand on her pregnant belly. Whenever I think of Rhiannon, I think of warm summer days, stability and a calm soothing voice. She is a wonderful deity to welcome into your space if you are looking for deep inner peace and grounding. Take her hand and feel her bring you back down to earth.

Elementals

So far, I've been talking about the elements, but each element has a mythical creature – or nature spirit – attached to it called an elemental. An elemental being is just another term for one of the infinite numbers of otherworldly beings, usually inhabiting a different but parallel plane of existence to ourselves.

Elementals are ruled by the element and embody its characteristics. Above, I have said 'mythical' creatures but anyone with second sight or who is particularly attuned to magickal workings will know that these creatures are very real.

The four main types of elementals are gnomes, fairies/faeries, salamanders and undines/mermaids. Tales of these nature spirits have formed an abundant tapestry over the years and there are few cultures across the world that do not have their own names for these beings. We've all heard about people getting transported off to Fairy Land when they stand in a circle of mushrooms, never to return, and mermaids sunning themselves on rocky outcrops just off the coast.

In the sixteenth century, the Swiss philosopher and alchemist Paracelsus corresponded each of these beings to an element – Earth, Air, Fire and Water respectively.

Although it might be very tempting to lure out the elementals to sit in their beautiful, otherworldly presence, elementals are much more at home on their own intersecting plane and should be treated with respect and observed from a distance.

So, why am I mentioning elementals here?

Elementals exist everywhere, just beyond our reach, and may appear to you in the course of your witchcraft practice. I do not advise working with them directly, especially if you are just beginning your witchcraft journey, but are ways to garner their favour that can work out to your advantage.

Let's talk about the Earth element and the elementals that accompany it.

Earth elementals

WE ALL KNOW what a gnome looks like, right? Pointy red hat, fluffy Father Christmas beard and a fishing rod?

Well, you might be surprised at how much gnomes look like knobbly potatoes. These short, 'earthy-looking' beings have a name that comes from the Latin *gnomus*, meaning 'earth-dweller', as they reside in mines, caves and burrows deep inside the earth.

Gnomes embody all the qualities of Earth and can be communicated with when a magickal practitioner is seeking stability, calm, resilience, a sense of loyalty, or a return to earthly pleasures. However, gnomes are also host to the more negative qualities associated with Earth including stubbornness, insensitivity, stagnancy and greed. It's because of this that I wouldn't advise working with them directly but instead allow their healing qualities to penetrate the atmosphere around you or a particular area from afar.

To welcome in the positive effects of the gnomes, we can show them a bit of kindness. Put yourself in the good books of the Earth spirits by:

+ tending your garden and filling it with wild or native flower species

+ creating a rockery

+ leaving them offerings of interesting stones (like a hag stone – with a hole in it), earthy-smelling herbs and shiny, beautiful things

+ sitting on the earth and sending well wishes and gratitude to the land.

By treating the Earth spirits well, you will start to notice their subtle positive influences in your life. Even though we can't always see their physical forms, the qualities of the Earth element will start to weave themselves into your life because you are in their favour.

Honouring the Earth element

As I have mentioned before, all of the elements deserve our respect, care and attention. In the case of Earth, there are many ways we can welcome this element into our lives and give thanks to it:

+ spending time outdoors barefoot

+ gardening using natural methods

+ carrying crystals such as: jasper, tiger's eye or smoky quartz

+ drinking herbal tea containing Earth-element herbs

+ wearing colours such as green or brown

+ drawing pentagrams around your home or wearing them as jewellery (see page 77 for more on pentagrams)

+ grounding yourself by kneeling down, flattening your body forward and placing your forehead on the floor – in yoga, this is called Child's Pose

+ looking for the earth placements in your astrological birth chart.

However, I find that one of the most grounding practices can be to create a shrine dedicated to the Earth element and mindfully choose items to place within it.

Creating an Earth altar

To honour the Earth element on your altar, you can:

+ add natural objects such as fallen twigs, pine cones or conkers

+ include fresh flowers but be mindful of where they come from. Perhaps dry out your own bouquet of flowers so they can be used year after year

+ prop up Tarot cards from the suit of pentacles

+ add an offering of nourishing food such as apples or oats

+ carve the Earth symbol into candles or create it out of natural objects

+ place the altar in a space that means you have to look northwards towards it.

Pentacles and pentagrams

The pentagram is a witch's symbol through and through. However, the five-pointed star encircled by a simple band has always been a spiritual symbol and was, believe it or not, at one point used to symbolise Christ on the cross. It has its origins in pre-history, with many ancient cultures using its perfect symmetry and geometric pattern to represent their different beliefs.

The Greek prefix 'penta', meaning 'five', encapsulates the star's five arms, but in Ancient Greece itself the pentagram was linked with the goddess of health. In the 1500s, the alchemist Heinrich Cornelius Agrippa associated the four elements with its arms, plus the mystical fifth element of 'aether'. These days in Neo-Pagan circles, that same fifth point of the pentagram – usually the arm at the top – often stands for the self or the soul, so that our spiritual selves are included in this beautiful ritual symbol.

While the pentagram can be seen as representing all the elements, it is ruled over by the element of Earth, with all its associations. In the art of Tarot, the suit of pentacles is centred around the home, hearth, money and earthly tangible possessions.

The terms 'pentacle' and 'pentagram' are often used interchangeably in witches' circles, but if we want to be technical about it:

☆ **Pentacle is a five-pointed star.**

⬠ **Pentagram is an encircled five-pointed star.**

You can use the pentagram as a symbol within your spellwork but you can also draw it on your notebooks, stitch it into the hem of your clothing and use lemon juice to outline it over your front door to bring groundedness and stability to your life.

Earth rituals and spells

This collection of spells and rituals is intended to help you ground your energy, release anxiety into the earth and use the nurturing power of the earth below us to heal, nourish and re-root ourselves.

Ritual for drawing self-love from the earth

LET'S START WITH self-love. I see self-love as the first step to complete healing – once we acknowledge to ourselves that we want to get better and recover from the experiences life has thrown at us, we can truly begin to embody that positive, motivational energy. Self-love is an empowering feeling that brings us stability and helps us walk with our heads a little higher than before.

Earth is such a nourishing healing element, so for this ritual we will be calling on its powers and melding with its energies to soak up self-love through our beautiful feminine roots.

You'll need:

+ a space large enough to lie down in

+ 4 pink candles

+ matches/a lighter

+ candle douter

+ a journal and pen

+ your ritual tools (see page 45).

1. Cast a circle, invoking the elements and any deities you wish to bring in, clearly stating your intention: 'I wish to draw self-love energy up from the Earth.'

2. Light a candle at each point of the compass then lie down (carefully!) in the middle of the circle.

3. For this ritual, you want to make sure that every possible point of your body is pressing into the ground – so spend some time adjusting yourself and pressing the back line of your body into the floor. Put one hand on your belly and one on your chest when you are comfortable.

4. Visualise your body sinking just below the surface of the earth's crust so that, in your mind's eye, your body is half-submerged in the earth below you. How would it feel to be so grounded and deeply rooted in the earth?

5. Think about projecting your consciousness outside of yourself and sinking it down very far into the ground (just like we did with the oak tree meditation on page 65). The ground is filled with leaves and organisms, pulsing with life. There is so much richness here and your body is safe and held by the nourishing soil. You can breathe easily and everything is filled with a nourishing darkness.

6. In the black womb space of the earth, you are safe. Safe to feel the world's heartbeat in this slow and soft place. In this cradle of safety, there is just you and the Earth element – an element filled with love and nurture.

7. Imagine the Earth element reaching out to you – putting a hand on your chest and pouring pink, loving light into your heart space. Soak this all up; feel it spreading like a soft palm throughout your body. It touches each of your fingers and toes, it raises up your chin and it brings a smile to your lips. This loving feeling is a secret between you and the Earth. Listen to any words that drift to you through the vibrations of the land and write these down later.

8. Take a deep breath and let this feeling settle into your body. Stay here, held, protected and cared for, for as long as you need.

9. Slowly, bring yourself back to your normal, everyday consciousness and feel the lightness in your face, shoulders and chest. You are now filled with love and know that you are always being looked after by Mother Earth. Say, 'I am filled with love,' and, as you snuff out the candles, say, 'So mote it be.'

10. Close your circle and journal about what you have just experienced. Make sure to spend as much time as possible outside today.

<hr />

Protecting your energy with apples spell

OVER THEIR LONG and powerful history, apples have gained many associations including wisdom, love, treachery and protection. Ancient Druids would have possessed a staff or wand made of one of two kinds of wood – yew or apple, both protective trees. This protective energy is one we'll be tuning into here.

Our own pattern of energy is unique to us and we often need to protect it from outside forces. In environments filled with jangly technology, heated meetings and frustrated co-workers, we often need to put up a barrier between us and the outside world. The charm bag in this spell is designed to help keep your own energies close while keeping negative energy from others at bay.

Apple folklore

In Arthurian legend, the land of eternal youth, Avalon, was a gateway to the Celtic underworld, 'Annwn', and that word comes from the Welsh for 'The Isle of Apples'. Some tales say that to enter Annwn, you needed to use an apple branch as a key.

Apples are the perfect component of protective magick: cut them in half and you'll see their seeds form a perfect pentagram – a grounding, protective symbol.

You'll need:

+ a large apple

+ a bay leaf

+ a small patch of earth or a plant pot filled with soil (if using the latter, this soil could be gathered from a place where you feel especially calm and safe)

+ a small black velvet drawstring bag

+ a sharp knife

+ a toothpick

+ a black candle

+ a small plate (that you can easily remove wax from)

+ matches/a lighter

+ as we will be performing protective magick, I suggest wearing the colour black in some form.

1. Clear a space for your magickal working on or near to your altar and cleanse the area.

2. Close your eyes and take a few deep breaths before lighting your black candle.

3. Lift the candle and drip a small circle of wax onto a cold plate. When the wax has cooled slightly, use the toothpick to draw a pentagram, starting at the left-hand bottom corner. Allow this to cool throughout the next part of the ritual.

4. Cut the apple in half and take a moment to observe the pentagram in its centre. Hold a half in each hand and say, 'Apple, fruit of the earth, protect me and keep me safe. Nothing can harm me; no negative energy can enter my space.'

5. Remove the pips from both halves and eat the portion in your right hand. Bury the left-hand portion in the plant pot or in your garden.

6. Take the apple pips, bay leaf and the now-solid wax pentagram and put these into your black bag. Hold it in your hands and visualise the bag being filled with a purple protective light, streaming from your hands. As you do this, say: 'Bay, apple, pentagram – protect me. Earth element – keep and bless me. Wherever I carry this charm, I will always be protected.'

7. Thank the divine energies for working with you today then cleanse the area. Keep the bag about your person to feel its protection all day long, put it near your front door to protect your home, or under your bed to protect you psychically at night.

Tip: *I recommend having a good stash of small fabric bags (see colour correspondences in the appendix on page 214). These things are infinitely useful in all sorts of different ways!*

Earth ritual for deep grounding

THIS RITUAL IS designed to stop the mind from racing and to get yourself back in your body.

You'll need:

+ your usual ritual tools

+ an outdoor space or a ground-floor room

+ optional: a tumble stone of smoky quartz, red jasper, tourmaline or hematite.

1. Purify your space, cast a circle and invoke Mother Earth or another Earth goddess you wish to work with. If you are bringing crystals into your ritual then place these in the north-facing direction of your circle.

2. Kneel down facing the north and set your intention, saying, 'Goddess, I invite you into my circle to centre and ground me.'

3. Visualise a root coming down from the base of your spine into the Earth. See it delving deep down into the ground below you or into the foundations of the building. This root has now attached you to the Earth: you are at one with it and can begin to soak up its energy. Stay here for five deep breaths, feeling the Earth's energy below your knees and pelvis.

4. We will now adopt three poses. For the first one, lean your torso over your knees so that your forehead is touching the ground and stretch your arms out flat in front of you so your palms are both touching the floor. Say, 'Goddess, I am grounded on the earth.' Stay here for at least 10 rounds of long slow breathing, visualising any jangly energy travelling through your Third Eye and your palms into the earth and becoming neutralised. The root from your spine brings in fresh healing energy to keep you stable.

5. Next, we move to standing, but bent forward and dangling at the waist so that our arms are swaying gently by our knees. Say, 'Goddess, I am balanced.' Stay here for at least 10 rounds of long slow breath, visualising any uncertain energy leaving you through your feet and the crown of your head. The root from your spine still pulses Earth energy into your body.

Earthing

Walking barefoot is a practice that has been used for millennia to help people connect their bodies to the earth. Sometimes known as grounding, earthing is said to fight depression, heart conditions and PTSD as well as improve sleep disorders and chronic fatigue, and its benefits can be felt after just 30 mins. But how does it work? It is thought that the earth's natural steady charge stabilises and levels out electrical currents in our bodies when it comes into contact with our bare skin.

After ritual work, you may feel 'buzzy' and wish to place your hands or forehead on the ground, allowing the heightened magickal energies to become neutralised by the earth.

6. Finally, move to a standing pose with your head held high and your arms ever-so-slightly away from your body. Say, 'Goddess, I am strong and centred.' Stay here for at least 10 rounds of long slow breath, visualising dark energy leaving through your feet and positive Earth energy absorbed through your root.

7. Once you have done this, make your way back to the ground into a kneeling position. Thank the Earth Goddess for sending you her energy and tell her how much you appreciate her kindness.

8. Close your circle then spend time walking in your garden (or around your house) barefoot to soak in even more of the Earth's energies. Leave an Earth offering in an outdoor space or perform an act to appease the Earth elementals today.

Panic attack prevention spell

THIS IS A charm to be performed in advance of an actual panic attack occurring. Those of us who have experienced panic attacks will know only too well the grip they hold on us once they get going so it is best to plan ahead to ensure your energies are grounded and stable from the offset. Scent is one of the major senses that can jolt us back to ourselves so this spell focusses on providing a grounding aroma to keep us inside our bodies.

You'll need:

+ 2 drops of patchouli essential oil

+ 2 drops of sandalwood essential oil

+ 1 drop of vetiver oil

+ 2 drops of wild orange oil

+ 1 small conker

+ 2 acorns

+ paper

+ pen

+ a small brown cloth bag

+ 10x10cm square of dark green cloth

+ brown thread

+ a needle.

1. In the centre of the green cloth, add the essential oils, conker and acorns.

2. On the pieces of paper, write a selection of words that calm and centre you. This could be things like 'Relaxed' and 'Grounded' or it could be actual

things that bring you joy and peace such as the name of your pet, 'Spending time in nature' or 'The Earth element'. Fold these up and add them to the centre of the cloth.

3. Bundle everything up and sew the edges of the cloth together so that it becomes a compact little package.

4. Bring the parcel to your nose and give it a big sniff before inserting it into the cloth bag. Carry the bag with you at all times and smell inside if you are starting to notice your anxiety creeping up. If the essential oils become faded over time, feel free to top them up by sprinkling them directly onto the cloth package.

Moving through fear ritual

WHERE DOES FEAR sit in your body? For me, it resides in my chest, over my heart, but for you this might be in the pit of your stomach or in your throat. Wherever this heaviness manifests inside of you, it's important to move fear through your system and outwards into the earth. Fear has the effect of drawing down your energy, lowering your vibration and rooting you to the spot; we want that fear to use its roots to burrow outside of you and leave your body, making sure that it doesn't plague you any longer.

You'll need:

+ a wide indoor space, preferably on the ground floor but this isn't absolutely necessary

+ a selection of white and black candles

+ a speaker, your phone or a CD player

+ an ecstatic dance playlist or lively music

+ your usual ritual tools.

Tip: *I recommend performing a cleansing ritual bath (page 178) before this particular ritual.*

1. Place your candles to fit the curve of your circle at the northwards-facing compass point.

2. Cast your ritual circle (including your music/speaker/device inside the circle), setting an intention to let go of fear. Light the candles in the north.

3. Making sure you are barefoot, put on your music and begin to dance, slowly at first, allowing your energy to rise. Begin with low movements around your hip and thigh area, bending at the waist and moving your belly.

4. Gradually, pick up the tempo so that you are moving more quickly. Bring your arms above your head and dance to your heart's content! Do this for as long as you wish.

5. Your energy is now elevated and flowing so you are going to shake it rapidly through your body. Do this by actually *shaking* yourself with gusto – this doesn't have to be in time with the beat: shake your fingers, your wrists, your shoulders, your face, your hair, your waist, your ankles and your toes. Stretch out your mouth and your forehead. You might even want to sing or let out single notes to feel the inside of your throat vibrate.

6. Now that your energy is raised and right at the surface of your body, you're going to stamp it out – you can apologise to the neighbours afterwards. With your feet flat, stamp the floor, releasing all of that pent-up energy into the earth. As your foot hits the ground, visualise any stagnant energy leaving you for good. Do this for as long as necessary.

7. It's time to calm the energy now. Slow down your shaking and dancing. You might be quite tired at this point so bring yourself down to a kneeling position to steady your breath then put your forehead on the floor. Say the words, 'I am

calm, I am without fear,' into the earth. Visualise a gorgeous, balmy energy rising into the space between your eyebrows, nourishing you with healthy energy to replace the stagnant energy you have released.

8. Close the circle and keep dancing at small intervals throughout the day.

5

Air

Uplifting, inspiring, energising

We all have an element that resonates with us the most and, of course, there is also the flip side of this. For me, the element of Air has never been 'the one'. Windy days and draughty corridors were a big no-no. When I first looked at my astrological birth chart, I was surprised to see a good mixture of Air signs in there so I started to delve a little deeper into what the Air element actually symbolised and entailed.

Air is the most cerebral of all the elements – when we relate it to the human body, it is all about the mind, our intellect and the inspiration that guides us. Perhaps this cerebral association is the reason I have historically clashed with Air. Air is the ruler of anxiety; when we experience anxious thoughts, our mind races, unhelpful words and sensations flying at us out of the dark, and we feel very ungrounded – not in our bodies. The 'airy' feeling of being steamrollered by our inner monologue isn't a pleasant one but there is also an abundance of positivity that comes with this element.

The element of Air is present in all our meditations, the words spoken in our spells and in our songs and chants, but also our deep breathing. Breathwork is a useful tool to learn how to harness the power of Air and is something we'll look at here. All of these Air-governed activities are proven to reset and heal the body. Recent research from the University of Bern in Switzerland into the vagus nerve, which runs from our heads through the centre of our torso and into the stomach, shows that this nerve controls our fight or flight response and can be regulated effectively through deep breathing, chanting or singing.[4]

Air is a masculine element, directly opposed to the feminine element of Earth. While Earth keeps us grounded in our bodies, Air helps us turn our consciousness outward. It tells us many things about the outside world: we might smell danger on the air, we might sense the winds of change blowing against us or it might bring us the comforting smell of freshly baked bread. When we learn to become still, we can feel what Air is trying to tell us.

I have recently found my favourite way to enjoy the Air element. If I find myself feeling overwhelmed, I will go outside on a grey and windy day and stand with my arms outstretched in my garden or a secluded spot in nature and feel the air buffet my body. I speak out loud any issues I wish to release to the wind and hear my voice carried off, far away from me. (For a variation of this, see the Depression blasting spell on page 118.)

But we must remember that Air can be calm as well – it isn't always a tornado. Still air can help us sit in the moment, can help birdsong to carry for long distances, and the gentle touch of a calm breeze can bring us back to ourselves when we are feeling blank.

So, let us take a deep breath and float into the element of Air.

Air correspondences	
Symbol	△
Direction	East
Zodiac signs	Gemini, Libra, Aquarius
Alignment	Masculine
Colours	Yellow, blue, white, grey, silver
Plants	Dandelion, lavender, peppermint, comfrey, eyebright, thyme, elder
Crystals	Clear quartz, citrine, calcite, fluorite, blue lace agate

Humour	Sanguine (warm and wet)
Moon phases	Waxing moon
Elementals	Sylphs, faeries, angels
Deities	The Anemoi/Venti, Vayu, Borrum, Njord
Tarot	Swords
Altar representations	Incense, feathers and the wand
Time of day	Dawn
Weekday	Wednesday
Heavenly bodies	Saturn and Mercury
Season	Spring
Opposing element	Earth

Guided meditation and breathwork for stillness in the mind and body

This guided meditation is ideal to do first thing in the morning to calm the mind or last thing before bed for a peaceful night's sleep. Read through it and memorise the key sections or record yourself saying the words so you get the full experience and don't have to look at this book. You can also download a recording of this meditation from jenniferlanewrites.com/meditations.

1. *Begin lying down or sitting in your favourite chair.
    Take a moment to get comfortable, making sure your
    weight is even on either side of your body. Allow your
    feet and ankles to release and become soft. Think
    about your tummy – you can release the muscles
    there now.*

2. *How do your arms feel? Flex your fingers a few times
    to release any tension. Now, draw your shoulders up to
    your ears and allow them to gently release. Last of all,
    scrunch up your face then let the muscles settle, keeping
    your jaw unclenched and the space between your
    eyebrows open.*

3. *When you're ready, come to stillness. You are feeling
    very comfortable exactly where you are. Your body is
    just the right temperature and you are ready to relax.*

4. *Begin to notice your natural breath through your nose.
    Is it deep or shallow? What kind of sound does it make?
    Is it affected or is it how you would normally breathe?
    On your next inhale, draw your breath down into your
    stomach area, allowing your stomach to rise on the in-
    breath and deflate on the out-breath. Do this for four
    more rounds of breath.*

5. *On your next inhale, continue to do your belly breaths
    but visualise the air entering your body as a bright
    white light. It is glowing softly and fills your lungs and*

belly with a soothing, balmy feeling. As you continue
with your deep breathing, imagine this light moving to
your arms and legs and up to the top of your head. This
light is connecting you to universal energy. Allow it to
fill you up and help you fall one step deeper into your
meditation.

6. Now that you are in a state of complete relaxation, you
   can start to use the breath to shift your awareness and
   clear your mind. We will now be doing some alternate
   nostril breathing. For this, we always begin on the left-
   hand side of the body – our feminine side – and end on
   the right – our masculine side.

7. Bring your right hand up to your face. Gently place
   your index and middle fingers on your Third Eye in the
   space between your eyebrows. Rest your thumb on your
   right nostril and your ring finger on your left nostril.

8. Hold your thumb down and inhale through your left
   nostril for the count of four – one, two, three, four.
   Now close both nostrils and hold the breath for one,
   two, three, four. Release the right nostril and exhale
   for one, two, three, four.

9. Now we'll go on to the right-hand side. Keep the left
   nostril covered and inhale through the right nostril
   for one, two, three, four. Close both nostrils and hold
   for four. Now uncover the left nostril and release the
   breath for one, two, three, four.

10. *Carry this breathing pattern on for three more full rounds. Your mind should now feel clear and alert.*

11. *If you haven't got the hang of this breath right away, don't worry. Find the rhythm that feels natural to you and you can always come back to this breath later on.*

12. *Now that we have focussed on the mind, it's time to go into the body and allow this calm to reach our core. For this next breath, if you feel comfortable, place your right hand on your heart and your left hand on your belly.*

13. *Begin by inhaling through your uncovered nose for the count of four, allowing this breath to make your belly rise. One, two, three, four. When you reach the top, hold this breath for four. One, two, three, four. Now, release the breath through your nose for the count of one, two, three, four. Inhale for four – one, two, three, four – hold for one, two, three, four, then release one, two, three, four. Carry on with this breath for a total of eight rounds.*

14. *This breath has now centred your body, grounding you in this hour, in this room and on this day. How do you feel now? Take a few moments to scan your body to notice any changes that might have occurred. Notice your breath starting to return to its normal pattern and speed. Wiggle your toes and fingers to bring yourself back into the present moment.*

15. *Take one final big belly breath through your nose, stretch out your arms and legs then exhale, bringing your hands back in so you can rub your upper arms. Lick your lips and blink your eyes open. You are now back in your bed or on your chair and ready for the next part of your day.*

Shadow work

Shadow work is the name we give to turning inward and mindfully reflecting on the darker parts of self.

We all have parts of ourselves that we're not so proud of – we might fly off the handle at the slightest hint of conflict or we might freeze when we need to speak up. While these self-parts might make us squirm and bring up unwanted feelings of embarrassment, sadness or even shame, if we don't work through them, they will always weigh on us and may even hold us back.

That's why working on our shadow selves is so important. Shadow work can be done through journaling, ritual work or speaking aloud to a mirror. I like to call it self-therapy. Parts of this process can be difficult, often bringing up negative past events and experiences. The result, however, will be a version of you that is more deeply in tune with your emotions, more stable and ready to put goodness and gratitude out into the world.

Air is the element of communication, and I am a strong believer that if we can communicate clearly and effectively with ourselves and understand our own wants and desires, then we are well on the road to healing.

What if my shadow work is taking too long to have an effect?

WORKING WITH ONE'S shadow takes time so don't be concerned if the process takes longer than you think. Gaining insight into the self is always valuable so try not to rush towards your healing goal as you are going through this process.

When should I practise shadow work?

AT ABSOLUTELY ANY time. Shadow work shouldn't just be reserved for times when we are feeling low – it is so valuable to know yourself so maybe you could weave shadow work into a regular journaling practice or something you do first thing in the morning to give yourself a strong sense of direction for the day. Many people like to practise shadow work during the autumn and winter months when the darkness outside encourages us to turn inwards and become more introspective. I find it very interesting that autumn and winter are months ruled over by Water and

Earth – the two feminine elements. Reflection, darkness and self-analysis are all things associated with femininity, as opposed to the traditional activity, solar energy and criticism of masculinity, so perhaps the darker seasons are the most appropriate times for shadow work but it's entirely up to you.

Is journaling shadow work?

IT CERTAINLY CAN be. We can write anything we like in our private journals or diaries and it's completely up to us how much we want to disclose in writing and how much we want to use writing as a tool to process our inner thoughts and feelings. Having a regular journaling practice is important as research shows that a mixture of writing, conversation and movement helps us to work through difficult events in our lives. When recovering from trauma or from a period of mental ill health, many professionals don't advise just taking one route (i.e. solely talking therapy) in their healing journey: a combination of the things I have mentioned above will help the body to process the event much more quickly and thoroughly – journaling can play a big role in that journey.

Journaling prompts

Below are 20 shadow work journaling prompts that will help you to gain deeper insight into your emotions and behaviours. By writing them down in your journal or notebook, you can reflect on them in a more meditative way and add any thoughts, resolutions or realisations that come up for you. Space these prompts out over the space of a month and return to them later in the year to see how far you've come.

Before you do this activity, make sure to have a calm mind. You may wish to drink a cup of peppermint tea to clear your head and pep up your mood, or you might want to do 5–10 minutes of meditation to put you in the right mindset for dealing with some challenging questions.

Once you're feeling ready, sit down with your journal to write down these questions and begin your shadow work. You might even want to create a protective circle around you to keep out negative energies while you do this.

1. How do I feel right now and where does that feeling sit in my body?

2. How do I react when I feel stressed or anxious?

3. Where do I seek comfort when I'm feeling this way and how do I self-sabotage?

4. Do I procrastinate and, if so, why is that?

5. If I don't complete the tasks I need to do in my day, what do I believe will happen?

6. What frightens me the most? And what would I do if this came to pass?

7. Do I judge myself harshly? How could I be kinder to myself?

8. When was the last time I cried or got angry? What was it about?

9. If I was going to go easy on myself tomorrow, what would my ideal day look like?

10. What am I holding on to? And where do I feel it in my body?

11. What three things am I most grateful for right now?

12. When was the last time I blamed myself for something that wasn't my fault?

13. What is my biggest regret? How has it changed the course of my life and how could I make peace with it?

14. If there were three things I could tell my past self, what would they be?

15. If I could cut ties with any person (or people) forever, who would that (or they) be and why?

16. Do I feel guilty about anything in my life? What is it and why does it make me feel this way?

17. What am I avoiding saying or doing?

18. What do I prioritise the most in my life?

19. How do I practise self-care? How often do I do it?

20. How could I love myself more?

After your shadow working session, make sure to treat yourself with kindness. You have been working through a lot so you could take a bath, go for a walk or put on your favourite music and dance around to bring you back into your body and let your mind gently process things in the background.

Herbs and plants associated with the Air element

I have found that herbs linked with the Air element often lend themselves to being burned as incense or as smoke-cleansing sticks – they also have powerful, memorable scents that you can imagine drifting to you on the breeze of a summer's evening.

Sage (*Salvia officinalis*)

IN RECENT TIMES, sage has become synonymous with cleansing. Its pungent leaves are often burned to purify an area but this is not its only virtue.

This slightly furry green garden herb has long been associated with deep wisdom. A 'sage' is someone who holds hidden knowledge and so this plant can be used to uncover answers to important life questions. Burn sage when you are seeking the truth and want to reveal a concealed pathway – meditate and listen to what lessons sage wants to impart.

Magickal properties: purification, repelling negativity, attracting positivity, wisdom, gaining knowledge

Meadowsweet (*Filipendula ulmaria*)

POSSIBLY THE MOST beautiful-smelling plant of all, meadowsweet is one of my favourites. It was once sacred to the Druids (that scent *is* rather heavenly) and has traditionally been used as an anti-inflammatory to treat arthritis, gout and joint swelling/pain. It can be drunk in teas and is also used as a diuretic to ease bladder and kidney infections.

Spiritually, meadowsweet symbolises peace, happiness and inner strength, all bountiful qualities. Pick fresh meadowsweet from meadows (of course), swampy areas or by the side of rivers and canals. Don't forget to leave plenty for the bees, who adore this scent just as much as we do.

Magickal properties: abundance, peace, happiness, contentment

Mint (*Mentha*)

STIMULATING AND INVIGORATING, mint is another plant with a sweet scent. Mint is a classic remedy for indigestion so always try a mint tea first if you're experiencing nausea. It has also been used to treat eye conditions due to its high vitamin A content and can be added to a bowl of boiling water to ease nasal congestion. Overall, it's just a great helping hand of a plant!

If you grow mint in your garden, you'll know just how hardy it is and how plentiful it can become when left to its own devices. As a result, mint represents abundance as well as prosperity, making it a good herb to use in times when you are feeling depleted and in need of a change in circumstance.

Magickal properties: prosperity, abundance, love, protection, health, inspiring action/energising, wellbeing

Smoke cleansing

Cleansing an area or object with smoke is an ancient practice seen across almost all cultures and on almost every continent including North America, Australasia, Africa and Europe. Even the Catholic Church loves a bit of incense. First Nation Tribes in North America often perform the act of smudging, which involves burning resins and sacred herbs such as white sage in a ceremonial way, but burning herbs for purification can be seen all across the world and is very common in the witchcraft community.

This practice is done by lighting dried herbs and then blowing or wafting out the flame so that the plant continues to smoke, releasing its aromas. This smoke can then be fanned around a person, object or space. By burning plants and releasing their medicinal and spiritual properties into the air, a space becomes imbued with these properties. Cleansing is an important act as it rids an area of negative energy or any residual energy left by a particular person or event. You may wish to perform a smoke cleansing on a room (or yourself) if you have come into contact with a draining or angry person, making sure their energy is eradicated and replaced with that of a sweet-smelling herb.

Scientific studies have shown that smoke cleansing with sage actually has antiseptic qualities and purifies the air by ridding it of bacteria – gargling with sage tea is great for getting rid of a sore throat!

Smoke cleansing has the added benefit of making us more mindful of our breathing and is, therefore, useful to release anxiety and lift the mood.

Some other popular herbs and plants used in smoke cleansing include:

+ sage

+ juniper

+ bay

+ rosemary

+ mugwort

+ thyme

+ lavender

+ cedar

+ spruce/pine.

How to dry herbs

Growing and collecting herbs is all part and parcel of being a green witch. You may wish to pick your own herbs to use as part of your magickal practice. If you are looking for herbs in the wild, always make sure to have an ID guide with you at first and look for three points of identification – for example, leaf shape, scent and petal number. Once you have gathered your herbs:

1. Leave your herbs on a clean surface for around two hours – this will give chance for any insects that have been resting on the plants to leave the vicinity of their own free will.

2. Wash the plants and pat them dry with a towel.

3. Using natural twine or kitchen string, tie them into small bundles and hang them up somewhere warm and dry. If the plant is particularly delicate – such as meadowsweet – you may wish to tie the plant inside a paper bag to keep the flowers from falling to the floor.

4. Leave the plant drying out for 2 weeks before use.

How to make a smoke-cleansing stick

BURNING HERBS BUNDLED into a long thin shape makes a perfectly holdable tool for cleansing your home or altar.

1. Gather together a bunch of herbs that is about 30cm long and about 8cm in diameter.

2. Divide the bunch into two strands and wind them around each other so they form a strong stick.

3. Secure the herbs together with a natural piece of garden twine then leave this to dry out for at least six weeks.

4. Burn the herb stick from one end by lighting it with a match or lighter. The dried herbs will initially produce a small flame – blow this out so that the end is smouldering slightly and smoking.

Tip: *When smoke cleansing a room, hold the stick over a fireproof dish. Make sure to leave windows and doors open to help the smoke escape and carry any negative energy away (as well as averting sudden fire alarm activity).*

Tip: *If you wish to cleanse yourself, you can do this by holding the burning herb and wafting its smoke with a cloth or handheld fan so that you get touched by the smoke from all directions.*

Air goddesses and gods

I actually want to talk about four deities this time – the Anemoi, or the four wind gods, who represent the element of Air:

+ Boreas, god of the north wind.

+ Eurus, god of the east wind.

+ Notus, god of the south wind.

+ Zephyrus, god of the west wind.

Although collectively they are the Ancient Greek Anemoi, individually they each rule over a different direction of the wind, and therefore a different season (winter, spring, summer and autumn using the order above). This means you can invoke a different member of the Anemoi depending on what season you are in, with each having a different, unique personality. I believe that this aspect of the Anemoi perfectly represents the changeability and suddenness of the Air element – the wind never blows in the same direction for long. Work with the Anemoi when you wish to bring change and transformation into your life.

Air elementals

Let's talk about the Fae.

Faeries, fairies, the Fae Folk, the little people – they come with many names and in different shapes and sizes. We might be most familiar with their depiction as delicate sprites that spring from branch to flower with a flutter of their wings, which is a fitting form of movement for an Air elemental. But the Fae are not always the sweet and whimsical fairies drawn by Cicely Mary Barker or peppered in the forests of Ferngully. Many a tale tells of people getting lured into a fairy ring (a natural circle of mushrooms) or enticing fairies into their home, only to be whisked away to another world across an airy veil, never to be seen again. Those who do manage to find their way back re-enter the world several decades or centuries later only to be driven mad by the fact that all of their loved ones are dead or no longer remember them.

If by some chance you do find yourself among them, never eat their food because this ties you to their land forever.

With this in mind, why (the hell) would you ever willingly choose to work with these Air elementals? Well, because faeries have a beautiful light, appealing energy: they value wit, hidden knowledge, cleverness and long memory. As with any elemental, you don't want to be in their bad books but their good side is very attractive and charming – filled with joy and a welcoming energy that will lift your spirits and make your face break out in a smile.

The positive effects of the Fae will be drawn to you if you:

+ leave them milk and sweet treats on your windowsill

+ hang wind chimes and other instrumentals that make a beautiful sound when the wind blows – use these sparingly as you obviously don't want to annoy the neighbours, but perhaps hang these up on a day that is special to you or when you are in need of some spiritual cleansing and take them down again at the end of the day

+ plant hawthorn and blackthorn trees that have airy, white blossoms in the spring

+ wear sweet-smelling perfume or burn oils and incense on windy days to carry the scent

+ think positive thoughts when out in the woods; they will know if you are bringing negativity into their space.

If you do decide to work with the Fae, you can have a long and rewarding bond that brings the delightful qualities of Air into your world. Be kind, thoughtful and respectful and you shall receive it back in abundance.

Honouring the Air element

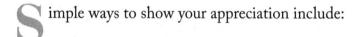

Simple ways to show your appreciation include:

+ wearing the colours yellow, blue, white, grey or silver

+ waking up in the morning and performing 10 minutes of breathwork before you start your day

+ singing, chanting or reciting verse

+ communicating clearly with your loved ones

+ delving deep into researching a subject that's dear to your heart to gain further knowledge and see what it inspires

+ opening your windows to let fresh air in

+ keeping plants indoors to purify the air

+ looking for the air placements in your astrological chart.

Creating an Air altar

+ Light incense

+ add Tarot cards from the suit of Swords

+ collect fallen feathers, wash them well, and include them in a △ shape

+ cleanse the area with smoke or by using a sound bowl

+ play your favourite music or soothing vibrations to add positive frequencies to the space

+ face the altar in an eastward direction.

Air rituals and spells

Working closely with the Air element in our spells and rituals can help to release anxiety or any stagnant feelings swirling inside your head. Harness this energy to bring in wisdom, focus and clarity, and move through periods of tiredness and procrastination.

Depression blasting spell

THIS ONE IS best performed on a windy day! Feeling depressed or experiencing sustained low mood can create stagnancy in our bodies – we move less, change our eating and sleeping habits, and our thought processes often become slower as if we're wading through mud to get to where we need to be. This spell can also be used to blast away common symptoms of burnout such as fatigue and brain fog. Air is the perfect element for blowing this sluggish energy out of our systems to welcome in something new.

While I recommend using a windy day to add potency to this spell, any form of breeze will generate power in this practice.

You'll need:

✦ **a windy hillside or field**

1. Find yourself in the space, taking long deep breaths and planting your feet firmly about hip distance apart. Hold your arms outstretched from your body in a strong, active standing pose. Feel the wind across your face and the power behind it.

2. As loudly as you feel comfortable, say in a commanding voice, 'Depression be gone. Sadness be gone. Air take it away – this is all done.'

3. Open your arms, eyes and mouth wide (don't be afraid of how you look!) and take in the biggest breath you can. Take three powerful breaths in and out and then inhale once more.

4. As you breathe out, bring your arms together so that your hands clap together loudly.

5. Do this several times, allowing your body to feel the resonance of the clap in the air before the wind carries it away. This action is just for you so don't be shy; allow Air to really take hold of you.

6. The wind will start to carry the stagnant energy in your body away. Once you feel this has happened (do you sense a lightness in your chest?), stop and say, 'Thank you, Air, for your blessing of movement. So mote it be.'

New moon manifestation ritual for a happy outcome

MANIFESTING IS BEST performed on a new moon and uses all the elements to help your wishes on their way. However, I see manifesting as especially connected with the Air element due to its association with the mind and visualisation.

But what is manifestation? Manifestation is using pinpoint focus and visualisation to bring our desires into reality. By completely embodying the sensation of our wishes coming to fruition and by sending out powerful streams of energy, we can redirect the course of events in our favour. For example, if my current job was giving me nightmares and I was struggling to find a new position, I might manifest a new role into reality using the method below.

Before you begin your manifestation ritual, take some time to really think about what you want the outcome of your ritual to be. Then think about how a particular outcome might make you feel – for example, if you did get that new job, how would that feel inside your body? Might you feel elation pulling up the corners of your mouth? Relief flooding your chest? Maybe a giddy buzz makes you want to hop around the room, followed by a deep sense of achievement. Feel all these things in your body, visualising the event happening as if it had already come to pass.

You can use a single ritual to manifest many different things but it is best to stick to between one and three things so that you can focus your energies in the most direct way.

You'll need:

+ your usual ritual tools

+ 1 white candle

+ 1 stick of selenite (a self-cleansing stone)

+ a scrap of paper

+ pen

+ matches/a lighter

+ a cauldron or a large fire-proof dish.

1. On the new moon, cast a circle and light a white candle. Instead of inviting a deity into your space, invite the moon to join you and bring in her beautiful energies.

2. State your intention, which is to ask the moon for her help in manifesting happiness into your life.

3. On the pieces of paper, write down the things you are hoping to bring into your life. This could be, 'I am starting a new job,' 'I have regained my social life after a period of depression' or 'I feel like myself again.' Whatever you write down on the paper, make sure to present them as 'I am' or 'I have' statements as if they were already happening in your life. This sends a clear message to the Universe.

4. Take the stick of selenite and hold this to your chest with your left hand. Pick up one of the manifestations with your right hand and say what is written on the paper three times.

5. Close your eyes and visualise your manifestation coming to pass. How would it feel? What good things would it lead to? How big would your smile be?

6. Now, hold the stick of selenite in the air with your left hand and burn the paper with your right hand

into the cauldron or a dish. Your intention will be channelled through your body and up into the ether through the selenite.

7. Do the same actions for anything else you wish to manifest today.

8. Once you have finished, thank the moon profusely and say, 'So mote it be'.

9. Close your circle and dispose of the ashes safely by putting them down the drain or burying them outside.

10. In the coming days, you may wish to write down your manifestations in a journal and meditate on them to keep them fresh in your mind and focus.

Full moon 'letting go' ritual

AS I MENTIONED above, the new moon is a time of manifesting new things into our life. However, at the full moon we release and let go.

This is a time of the month to think about all the things in your life that no longer serve you and do not add positivity to your life – for example, a relationship with a particular person that is dragging you down, a dead-end job or feelings of inadequacy that we might have in ourselves that are holding us back. We are clinging on to these things, energetically. However, the power of the moon can help us to undo our grasp on them and let them go so that we can move on to bigger and better things.

You'll need:

+ **your ritual tools**

+ **1 white candle**

+ **several scraps of paper**

+ **pen**

+ **matches/a lighter**

+ **a cauldron or a large fire-proof dish.**

1. Cast your circle, lighting the white candle, and invite the moon's energies to join you this evening. You may wish to do this outside or in a place where you can see the full moon from a window.

2. State your intention out loud – to let go of people, memories and situations that no longer serve you in your life and which are holding you back from achieving health and happiness.

3. On scraps of paper, write down what you wish to release. Write them as statements or phrases – the clearer the better. For example, 'I release resentment

over [a situation]', 'anxiety and worry' or 'my attachment to [a specific person].' You can release as many things as you wish but, to focus your energy, it is best to choose up to three, or just one.

4. Look up to the moon and ask her to help you release what you have written down.

5. Taking the first piece of paper in your hands, read what it says aloud three times. Then close your eyes and visualise the full moon's gaze hitting your Third Eye (the space between your eyebrows) and melting this thing energetically out of your system: as you breathe in, imagine inhaling the moon's pure white light. The light courses through your body, turning the negativity you feel around this statement to pure brightness. When you exhale, visualise your breath taking away any leftover negativity energy, sinking it into the ground and leaving your system cleansed. Take notice of how this feels. How have your feelings changed? Where do they sit in your body? Think about how your life will be different now that this situation is no longer in your life.

6. Next, burn the paper in the cauldron with the flame from your white candle, using this as another opportunity to visualise the feeling leaving your body. Once there are only ashes left,

the thing that had been written on the paper will no longer be a part of you.

7. Repeat steps 5 and 6 with any other pieces of paper. When all are burned, say, 'So mote it be.'

8. Stay in the circle for as long as you want, meditating on what you have just released.

9. Close your circle, give thanks to the moon and spend some time moon gazing before coming back to reality.

10. After your ritual, be sure to bury the ashes in the ground to neutralise any residual energy.

Growing your joy spell jar

SPELL JARS ARE a beautiful, compact way of working magick.

I find spell jars and charm bags particularly useful within spellcraft as they are visual representations of a spell. Sometimes, it is easy to perform a piece of magick and practically forget about it the next day once we're back in work mode. However, with a spell jar or bag, we can keep this about our person or in our house as a constant reminder of the spell we worked.

This particular spell jar will bring happiness and contentment to your life.

You'll need:

+ a small sterilised glass vial (sterilise a clean vial by filling it with hot salt water for 20 minutes or by putting it in the oven at 180 degrees for 15 minutes)

+ 5 dried dandelion heads

+ 2 tsp of Himalayan salt

+ 2 tsp of dried lemon balm

+ 1 tsp of dried peppermint

+ 1 tsp of lavender

+ 1 stick of lavender incense

+ a yellow candle

+ matches/a lighter.

1. Light the incense and, when it is smoking, insert this into the vial and move it around three times in a clockwise motion. Then do the same to the outside of the vial, including its stopper.

2. Add the salt to the bottom of the vial.

3. Then, starting with the heaviest plant/herb, place each one inside. This does not have to be neat but, as you are adding the plants, repeat the intention of your spell jar under your breath using words such as 'I am filled with joy.'

4. Visualise that joy as yellow light glowing in the centre of your body. With each breath you take while completing this spell jar, feel the light inside you growing brighter.

5. Once the vial is filled to the brim, light the candle and allow its wax to melt. Drip the wax into the opening of the vial and insert the cork or stopper. Continue to drip the wax around the stopper and on top of it so the jar is completely sealed by the wax.

6. Allow to cool and keep the jar with you or in a place where you will see it every day, such as by the front door, to remind you of the joy that is winging its way to you.

Wind-in-your-sails pinpoint focus spell

WHEN WE ARE overwhelmed, it is very common to feel scattered and a bit all over the place. This can have a negative impact on other areas of our lives, forcing us to miss appointments and not reply to our friends. This crystal anointing spell cuts through the overwhelm to bring clarity and focus back to our minds, allowing us to get on top of things again, which is sometimes the first step to mastering our burnout or emotions.

You'll need:

✦ 1 large chunk of calcite or citrine cleansed in the light of the full moon or by using sage smoke

✦ 1 tsp of dried mint

✦ 1 tsp of dried sage

✦ 1 tsp of dried rosemary

✦ grapeseed or olive oil

✦ a small dish

✦ a white cloth bag or a piece of muslin

✦ a tea towel.

1. Create the anointing oil by mixing the three herbs with the oil (see page 142) inside the dish and stir it three times in a clockwise direction.

2. Take your crystal and anoint it with the mixture so that the crystal is entirely covered.

3. Hold the crystal up to natural light and look at the colour and light shapes it emits.

4. Bring the crystal to your Third Eye – this will mean that some of the oil also anoints your forehead – and say: 'Element of Air, with your piercing stare. I am under your gaze, lift this haze. Focus my mind, everything is now clear.'

5. Keep the crystal there for as long as you feel is necessary to soak up its energies. Breathe deeply as you do this. Then put the crystal on a clean towel in front of an open window, allowing it to air dry for a day or two.

6. Once the crystal is dry, put it in the white bag or wrap it in the muslin cloth and carry it with you or put it in your place of work.

Feather charm bag to dispel heavy feelings

EVER FEEL LIKE you're carrying the weight of the world on your shoulders? Feelings of overwhelm and sadness can often have a heaviness to them – whether you feel it in your chest, your stomach, your mind or your shoulders. This charm bag uses herbs, incense, colours and symbols associated with the Air element to lift those feelings and carry them away.

You'll need:

+ 2 white feathers

+ 1 small white or pale blue bag/pouch

+ 1 lavender incense stick

+ 2 tsp of dried peppermint

✦ 1 needle

✦ white thread

✦ matches/a lighter.

1. Take your bag and stitch the universal symbol for Air onto one side △ .

2. Fill the bag with the two feathers and the dried peppermint.

3. Light the incense and allow its smoke to land on the bag and its contents. As you do this, say aloud, 'Charm, lighten the air around me; when I carry this pocket, I am free.'

4. Visualise yourself with your shoulders drawn back; nothing is holding them down. Your chest and abdomen are light and expansive as you hold the bag in your hands. The air around you is a crackling blue fizz, preventing any negative energy from touching your body.

5. When you have visualised for however long you need, sew up the edge of the bag/pouch to keep its contents inside and carry the charm with you whenever you need it.

6

Fire

Passionate, cleansing, motivational

I'd like to say the reason I love fire is because my star sign is Aries (the cardinal fire sign). However, it's more likely that my mum told me to never light candles in my room and I'm a rebel at heart.

Despite the well-known destructive effects of fire, fire can also be soothing. A candlelit bath in an otherwise dark room can allow us to remain mindful as we soak. Watching the reflection of the flames dance and play on the water is an infinitely more enjoyable pastime than scrolling through our phones. We all know that watching a crackling log fire has a completely mesmerising effect – perhaps because it connects us with our ancestors, who would have sat around a fire, looking for shapes in its red-hot tongues and telling stories about the creatures they saw in it. There is something about Fire that is so human and timeless, perhaps more so than the other elements.

Why might this be? Tangible flames do not tend to exist without the input of human hands, unless they are caused by a rogue electrical storm or by intense summer heat. We can close our eyes and imagine our hunter-gatherer ancestors using the Earth element to conjure flames into being with the dexterous flick of a hand and a flint. The pride they must have felt when those first flickering embers fell onto the kindling and began to smoke. Fire was craved and wished for in order to feed the tribe and has been the focal point of meal times, sleeping arrangements and general comfort across time.

However, Fire is also ever-present in the form of the sun, something older than the Earth itself, linking us back to an unknown period of time when no human thought existed in the world.

In its most destructive form, Fire can rage through towns, cities and forests, stopping only in the face of its opposing element – Water. It can break and batter ecosystems that have taken millennia to develop, and vanish a lifetime of possessions in seconds. However, in its wake we often find creation.

Many plants, such as eucalyptus, actually require the element of Fire to melt the coat of resin from their seeds before they can fully germinate. From wildfire, the phoenix can rise.

Fire is an element that allows us to burn away our past selves and the imprints of any negative events that have brought us to where we are today. It strips those moments from our skin and sizzles them into oblivion. From its ashes, our true selves can emerge. Perhaps this sense of renewal and change is the reason I love it so much.

This element is ruled over by the south (where the warm winds originate), passion, creativity and motivation, making it the perfect element to rouse the senses and bring action into your life again after a period of inactivity, low mood and unwanted stillness. Fire will blast your old life away and honour you with a fizzing new burst of energy.

Fire correspondences	
Symbol	△
Direction	South
Zodiac signs	Aries, Leo, Sagittarius
Alignment	Masculine
Colours	Red, orange, gold, yellow
Plants	Nettle, rosemary, angelica, basil, garlic, hawthorn, calendula, rue

Crystals	Carnelian, citrine, clear quartz, gold, sunstone, amber, garnet, tiger's eye, bloodstone
Humour	Choleric (hot and dry)
Moon phases	Full moon
Elementals	Jin, Genies, Salamanders
Deities	Ogun, Agni, Brigid, Ra, Logi, Hestia, Helios, Vesta, Vulcan
Tarot	Wands
Altar representations/ tools	Athame and candles
Time of day	Noon
Weekday	Sunday and Tuesday
Heavenly bodies	The Sun and Jupiter
Season	Summer
Opposing element	Water

Herbs and plants associated with the Fire element

Rosemary (*Rosmarinus officinalis*)

FOLKLORE TELLS US that growing rosemary close to your front door will bring happiness and luck to the house. Not only this but the larger the rosemary bush grows, the more the woman of the house rules the roost. In the past, this has led to men chopping rosemary down but now is the time to let our rosemary grow!

Rosemary's ability to exist in very dry conditions is its first link with the Fire element. Its fiery nature helps to boost our circulation and rosemary has been commonly used as a hair mask for centuries as it stimulates the blood in our scalp to encourage healthy, fresh hair growth. This translates to its magickal properties as well and rosemary can be used to encourage mental and physical stimulation in times of depression and burnout, as it flushes out stagnant areas from the body and from any space that has dense or darker energies.

Magickal uses: fidelity and loyalty spells, removing stagnant energy, stimulation, invigoration, mental clarity, cleansing, protection

Calendula (*Calendula officinalis*)

ALSO KNOWN AS the marigold, calendula is beloved by many gardeners for its gorgeous golden face. But it is also a favourite of many witches who want to harness its beautiful solar energy. Calendula is ruled over by the sun and its fiery nature makes it the perfect addition to infusions and tinctures that promote happiness. It is also known for its protective qualities – possibly because its sunny face can be seen as lighting the way through dark times.

Another use for calendula is to bring out one's own physical beauty. When its petals are dried out and added to sweet almond oil, it can make a gorgeous ritual anointment oil that can be used in self-love and confidence magic. Calendula is also an anti-inflammatory, which can help the skin on a practical level.

Magickal properties: happiness, joy, confidence, protection, success/financial abundance and beauty

Nettle (*Urtica dioica*)

MUCH MALIGNED AND misunderstood, it makes me so sad that no one likes the stinging nettle!

Ruled by the planet Mars, getting stung by a nettle is like putting your hand in a flame – you definitely know about it once it's done. Nettle has many of Mars' attributes including its hyper-masculinity. As a result, it can be used to give you a boost of energy and power. If you are feeling deflated or defeated, then a little bit of nettle goes a long way. Every spring, I create a nettle vinegar that can be used on salads, which adds a bit of peppy Martian drive and energy, bursting out of our winter hibernation. I also love nettle because it is packed full of iron and is therefore brilliant for boosting the blood and battling anaemia.

Magickal properties: awakening, transformation, energy, setting boundaries, drive, action

Candle magick

By the light of a flickering candle, all our desires can be realised. Candles are a fantastic tool for manifestation, an active symbol of our desires and passions that can drive our intent into reality. So, candle magick is a must for witches and spiritual folk wanting to influence the outcome of their future.

When we light a candle, we can often find ourselves completely mesmerised by its swaying beauty, which can send us into a trance-like state and make it easier to connect with spiritual beings. The flame itself can be used in rituals and spells to represent the element of Fire; however, one of the beauties of candles is that they contain all four elements in one place:

+ **Earth:** The solid body of the candle.

+ **Air:** Oxygen is needed to feed the flame.

+ **Fire:** The flame itself.

+ **Water:** Melting wax as the candle turns to liquid.

With this in mind, candle magick can be seen as imbued with extra power. The flame can be used to burn away what no longer serves us but can also add fuel to an idea and cause it to come to fruition.

Where possible, try to enhance your workings with soy and beeswax candles – these are more environmentally friendly alternatives to paraffin wax and can be safely disposed of or composted, and will be looked upon more favourably by the Fire element.

Dressing a candle

Candles like dressing up – it helps their magick shine brighter.

Infusing a carrier oil with herbs or adding essential oils (see page 142) and smoothing it over the surface of a candle before spellwork is called 'anointing' or dressing a candle. Your anointment oil adds potency to any candle magick and guides the intention of any spell. As part of dressing a candle, you can also carve it with symbols, sigils or runes to enhance its properties. Below is how to anoint your candle for the best spell outcome.

1. First, choose the colour candle that corresponds with the magick you wish to work (see page 214).

2. Use a small, sharp object to carve any symbols or words into the candle's wax that will add to your spell. With anything you carve, make sure to start at the top of your candle close to where the wick is showing.

3. To anoint a candle, select an oil blend and put a small amount of the oil onto your hands. Rub this in so your fingers have a good coverage.

4. If you are using your spellwork for manifestation or welcoming a new energy into your life, rub oil onto the candle from the top to the middle and then from the bottom to the middle, gathering the energy into the centre of the candle.

5. If you are performing spellwork to burn away links with the past or banish any negative emotions, you will need to put the oil on in the opposite way: anoint the candle from the middle to the top and then the middle to the bottom, push the energies outwards and away from you.

6. You can also add herbs to the candle's body for extra potency and apply them in the same way as adding the oil above.

7. Once you have done this, you are ready to begin your official spell work as your candle is filled with energy and ready to go!

Make your own anointment oils

These essential oil blends are designed to create activating anointment oils for different kinds of spell work. Mix these with a small amount of carrier oil, i.e. grapeseed oil, sweet almond oil or olive oil, before you apply them to an object. As well as anointing candles, you can also use these oils in small quantities on your body, such as in the space between your eyebrows, your throat and your heart space.

The below oils can enhance your magickal working but they are not strictly necessary, especially if you are on a budget or looking to perform a spell or ritual in a hurry. They can also be made with fresh or dried herbs if you do not have access to essential oils.

+ **Protection** – 4 drops basil oil, 3 drops geranium oil, 2 drops pine oil, 1 drop vetiver oil.

+ **Physical healing** – 3 drops eucalyptus oil, 1 drop rose oil, 1 drop spearmint oil.

- **Mental healing** – 5 drops lavender oil, 5 drops eucalyptus oil, 5 drops orange oil, 3 drops rosemary oil, 2 drops pine oil, 4 drops sandalwood oil.

- **Banishment/cleansing negativity** – 5 drops pine oil, 4 drops rue oil, 3 drops peppermint oil, two crushed peppercorns.

- **Self-love** – 6 drops vanilla oil, 6 drops rose oil, 5 drops lemon oil, 6 drops jasmine oil, 5 drops orange oil.

- **Calm** – 3 drops ylang-ylang oil, 3 drops lavender oil, 2 drops chamomile oil, 1 drop rose oil.

Guided meditation for self-transformation

This guided meditation is best done on the new moon and is a wonderful way to harness the creative power of fire to transform your state of mind. When we have been stuck in one way of being for a long time, we sometimes need a spark to break us free, allowing us to reclaim our true selves. You will come out of this meditation feeling strong, more confident and in control. You can also download a recording of this meditation from jenniferlanewrites.com/meditations.

Before you begin, lie or sit down comfortably in a candlelit room, allowing the shadows to flicker against your eyelids. For this exercise, I would advise having a sprig of yarrow under your pillow. Yarrow is a herb often used in vision work and divination; in this visualisation, it will help to guide the energies towards the future to help manifest the transformation that will occur.

1. *You are warm and safe. Breathe in deeply into your stomach and hold the breath there for four, three, two one, then exhale slowly.*

2. *Visualise yourself in a familiar place that brings you joy. This could be a forest you go to when you want to spend time in nature, a lake where you have swum, your childhood garden, or somewhere else. Listen to the sounds of this place. Reach out and touch the nearest tree or plant, helping you to feel grounded in this space.*

3. *You notice something flickering on your right-hand side and turn towards it. There is an ethereal-looking staircase leading upwards. It has a candle on either side of each step and you can hear a crackling fire coming from a space at the top of the stairs. It makes you feel warm and calm.*

4. *You slowly climb the steps, counting them under your breath as you do so. Ten, nine, eight, seven, six, five, four, three, two, one. You are now at the top of the*

stairs and you emerge into an entirely new place you've never seen before.

5. *In front of you is a vast grassland stretching out so far that you can't see its edges. The sky is a dark violet colour, just before sunrise. There is a sense of anticipation in the air. But the air is pleasant and a gentle breeze plays against your arms. You see exactly where the crackling fire sound was coming from — further out in the grassland, you see a large bonfire in a clearing surrounded by stones. It is taller than you and is burning brightly. You make your way towards it and, as you get closer and closer, you start to feel the heat of the bonfire on your skin. It is so bright but you keep looking straight at it.*

6. *You're now standing directly in front of the fire facing east so that you can see the sun just starting to light the sky. The fire feels like a summer's day on your skin.*

7. *You look closer and see that something is moving inside the fire. It's a small version of you. This little you is made of bright light and is living inside the fire, moving with its ripples and undulations so they are dancing. Little you has their arms outstretched inside the fire.*

8. *This little version of you has already shed the past and is living in the present. All their worries have been burned away by the flames. What if you were to join*

them inside the flames; how would you feel? Free,
joyful, living?

9. You draw your body up very tall, your chin held high,
and you step inside the fire.

10. Surprisingly, the fire does not harm you. Yes, it is hot
and you can feel it against your skin but it does not
hurt you. You see the small version of yourself dancing
in front of you. They are beckoning to you and you
begin to dance just as they do with the rhythm of
the flames. As you watch the mini-you, you feel so
proud of their joy and strength, their ability to not
care about how anyone else perceives them. They are
completely at one with themselves and you know now
that you can be too.

11. You both dance close together until you are touching.
In a smooth, silky voice, the mini-you says, 'Are you
ready to let the past go? Are you ready to transform
your soul?'

12. With your chin high, you say, 'Yes, I am.'

13. Without pausing, the little flame version of you steps
inside your body. It fills you up, radiating to all parts
of your body: your feet, your thighs, your pelvis, your
stomach, your heart space, your forearms and hands,
your throat and your whole head. It is a wonderful
sensation; the waves of power washing over you,

burning away self-doubt, shame, anxiety or sadness. It is all gone and all that is left is this bright and shining version of you who is filled with power.

14. *Look down. What is that in your hand? It is a ball of light about the size of a golf ball. This is your offering to the Universe – a thank you for its guidance. As you look at it, the light begins to pulse and you can feel it growing between your palms until it is the size of a bowling ball. It is filled with power, just like you.*

15. *Throw the light up to the sky and watch it ascend into the Heavens, but before it is completely gone, reach up and grasp some of this light in your hands and press it to your chest, feeling it enter you and spread out inside your body.*

16. *Now, it is time to step out of the flames and head back to your safe, calm place. You walk out of the fire, through the grassland to the ethereal steps that will take you back home. The candles on either side of the stairs seem to glow brighter than they did before.*

17. *Your feet touch the ground and you are now back in your safe place. But things are different now. You are taller, stronger, and there is a smile playing about your lips. You have been transformed.*

18. *Spend time in this quiet space or open your eyes and enjoy your day.*

Fire gods and goddesses

Brigid (pronounced *Breed*) is a potent Fire goddess and I have often gone to her first when seeking deep healing in times of pain or need. But who is she? The goddess Brigid is from the Celtic pantheon of deities and is typically seen as the 'maiden' aspect of the Triple Goddess. Many Pagans worship the Goddess who embodies 'maiden, mother and crone' – each aspect of womanhood. Brigid, with her childlike excitement, is the ruler of poetry, spring, healing and sacred fire, making her a Goddess with a special affinity with candle magick.

Fire elementals

There are many different types of Fire elementals but perhaps the most commonly known is the salamander. Nope, not the amphibious newts that you might have come across, although this Fire elemental also takes a small, slithery lizard-like form.

The word 'salamander' comes from the Ancient Greek for 'fire lizard' and these elementals really do love the flames! Their skin is impervious to fire and they live their lives basking in fireplaces and volcanoes. Wherever there is fire, there is a salamander. Thinking back to times past when everyone had an open fire in their homes or in their local communities, people would have been able to observe salamander energy snaking over the log pile along with the tongues of the flames every day.

Salamanders embody all the qualities of Fire and can bring you renewed passion, courage and creativity. I have always been cautious about working with salamander energy as Fire is not always the simplest element to communicate with (fire loves to be a bit sassy and capricious) but there are many things you can do to welcome in the gorgeous, positive effects of salamanders:

+ **leave flat stones in your garden for them to bask on in the sun (just like slow worms or lizards)**

+ **amplify the light in your home with mirrors and gold decor**

+ **create a space for them on your altar, including red, orange and yellow crystals, hot spices and plenty of candles**

+ **raise your face up to the sun and give thanks to them.**

Once the Fire elementals can see your respect, you may start to notice passion, drive and motivation hurtling back into your life. Welcome in that fire and get comfortable in the light.

Honouring the Fire element

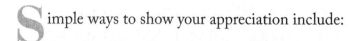imple ways to show your appreciation include:

+ lighting candles or a small fire outside

+ holding your face and arms up to the sun

+ growing sunflowers

+ carrying fire crystals like carnelian

+ wearing red, orange or yellow clothes with gold jewellery

+ looking for the fire placements in your astrological chart.

Creating a Fire altar

+ Light candles with fiery colours

+ add Tarot cards from the suit of Wands

+ place crystals or candles on a gold plate

+ yellow, orange or red candles will add potency

+ face the altar in a southward direction.

Fire rituals and spells

When I decided to quit the office job that had been making me ill, I harnessed the elements for their help. I did two rituals to release myself from the clutches of that environment – both rituals involved fire. The rituals reflected my emotions at the time: my flesh felt singed, like I'd just escaped a burning building and was now dealing with the aftershock. By using fire in my rituals, I was scorching a line in the ground between my past experience and my new self. The first two rituals here are the ones I performed.

In this book, I have included more rituals and spells for Fire than for any other element because, well, it's my favourite element, but also because I find Fire to be the most transformative and cleansing element and the one that has helped me in my personal journey the most. I hope you can gain the benefits of a warm flame fanning against your cheek as I have.

Fire cord-cutting spell to sever ties with a person or place

DURING THIS SPELL, it is key to keep a level head. There are obviously reasons why you want to sever connection with this particular person or place, but when we let anger come into our sacred space it enters the spell, and can often be magnified in strange and sometimes scary ways. Remember the words 'And it harm none do as ye will' when you perform this spell. Meditate beforehand to enter a calmer state if you feel like your emotions might run away with you.

To be performed on the night of a full moon.

You'll need:

+ around 30cm of black cotton thread or cord

+ a black candle

+ a pen

+ two small pieces of paper

+ matches/a lighter

+ two fireproof dishes

+ grapeseed oil

+ 1 teaspoon of dried rosemary

+ a trowel or small digging implement.

1. Cleanse the area using your preferred method.

2. Anoint the candle with the oil and rosemary and set up the fireproof dishes next to it.

3. Take a small piece of paper and write on it the

person, experience or event you want to cut free. On the other piece of paper, write your own name.

4. Fold the papers and tie them together with black thread or cord so the pieces of paper lie at either end of the thread.

5. Light the candle and, hovering the cord high above, say, 'With this flame, I cut the cord, I cut what lies between. With this flame, I cut the cord. Let me be at peace.' As you say this, visualise the bond between yourself and this person/ place disappearing, like you are strangers to one another.

6. Lower the thread into the flame, holding a name in each hand. It won't take long for the fire to sever the cord.

7. Once the thread is cut, burn the papers one at a time, making sure to keep their ash in separate fireproof dishes.

8. Visualise yourself healing and growing stronger as you look into the flame. Allow this fire vision to fill you up from head to toe with your chin held high.

9. Bury the ash outside in two separate spots then cleanse the area using your preferred method.

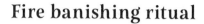

Fire banishing ritual

IF YOU FEEL like your cord-cutting magick needs to be amplified then perform this ritual to finally rid something from your life. This ritual is best performed on a Saturday and a waning moon.

You'll need:

+ 1 black candle

+ a candle holder

+ a toothpick or small carving implement

+ a pen

+ paper

+ a cauldron or heatproof bowl

+ matches/a lighter

+ banishment candle oil – dried rosemary, a few drops of pine oil, dried nettle, grapeseed oil

+ your usual ritual tools.

1. Cleanse the ritual space then cast a circle widdershins (anti-clockwise), starting in the west and invoking the elements in the reverse order to what you would do usually.

2. State the intention of your ritual out loud, saying who or what you wish to banish and what you want the outcome to be.

3. Anoint the candle using the banishing/letting go method.

4. Write the names or situations you wish to be rid of onto pieces of paper in an 'I banish ____ from my life' format. Fold each one into quarters.

5. Read aloud the things you wish to banish, one by one, and visualise what it will mean for you once these things are gone from your life. How will it make you feel? What new opportunities will arise for you? For each piece of paper you read aloud, carve a symbol, sigil or rune that signifies strength to you into the candle, starting near the top.

6. Burn each piece of paper in turn, visualising the smoke spiralling away into the top of your circle and being removed forever from your presence.

7. Leave the candle burning as you meditate on your newfound freedom. Do you feel lighter already?

8. Close the circle in a deosil (clockwise) direction, starting at the north, but keep the black candle burning.

9. Bury the ashes outside to neutralise them – do not keep them in the house for long.

10. Cleanse the space and keep the candle burning until either the sigils have melted away or the whole candle is burned.

Sunlight positivity magnification ritual

THIS RITUAL IS designed to magnify and grow positivity, confidence and assertiveness on our healing journey. By harnessing the power of the sun, we can enhance light and joyfulness in our lives.

This piece of magick turns its back on any areas of our lives attached to 'lack' or discontent. Instead, it shines its focus on areas where we are happiest and have the most gratitude. By honing in on and giving thanks for what we already have, the universe understands this as a signal that we are inhabiting an energetic space of abundance. When we are in this place of appreciation and plenty, we can allow joy to spill into *all* areas of our lives.

To be performed on a sunny day.

You'll need:

+ 1 yellow candle (to symbolise contentment and joy)

+ a toothpick or small carving implement

- paper
- a pen
- a shiny gold plate or a mirror
- your usual ritual tools
- matches/a lighter.

1. Set up and purify your ritual space, invoking any deities you might want to work with – you might wish to welcome in the mother goddess Rhiannon and have her watch over your ritual. If you do not wish to work with a deity then continue with the spell below.

2. Take your candle and carve a sun symbol into it (like this ☉) at the top. You can also add any sigils that represent abundance and gratitude to you.

3. Using a blob of candle wax, stick your candle (if using a taper candle) to the centre of your gold plate or mirror, or just stand it in the middle.

4. On small scraps of paper, write down all the things in your life that currently bring you joy. You might write down things like: 'My family makes me laugh so much,' 'I love walking by myself, it makes me feel free,' or 'My job makes

me feel fulfilled.' Be as specific as you want and write as many different gratitudes as you please. The more the merrier!

5. Burn the gratitudes in the candle flame one by one, visualising how each one makes you feel – really embodying that feeling so it fills you up and makes you smile. As you do this, repeat: 'The sun shines; so do I – three times, four times, multiplied.' Really take your time with this step, letting the feelings sink in.

6. As you do this, your smile will be reflected in the mirror/plate below the candle – doubling your joy and the confidence that comes alongside that inner happiness.

7. Close your ritual, giving thanks to the Goddess. Perhaps you could perform small acts of kindness in your local wild spaces (such as feeding the birds or watering a thirsty plant) for the rest of the day to take your gratitude even further.

Tip: *You might also bring in some herbs or plants that represent joy. Why not try creating a flower crown out of dandelions and wearing it for your ceremony?*

Fire-in-the-belly spell to combat dissociation

DISSOCIATION IS A common symptom of stress and anxiety and can often lead to unremembered lapses in time, procrastination and bodily numbness. Creating fire within the body can blast away any stagnancy and help to kick your brain into action once more. This spell can also be used to bring back our motivation and drive.

You'll need:

+ 1 large red candle

+ matches/a lighter

+ a candle douter

+ a cup of cinnamon tea with honey (steep 1 cinnamon stick in hot water for 10 minutes).

1. Sit in front of your cleansed altar space and light the red candle. Don't bring any technology or distractions into the area.

2. Drink your tea and watch the flame move in its natural way. Make a mental note of any observations that come up for you. Does the

flame remind you of anything? Do you see any shapes inside the fire? Stare into the flame, or watch its shadows, for as long as it takes you to drink your tea.

3. Once you have finished your tea, say the words, 'The fire burns inside me, it takes my fear and doubt. My spirit is a flame that can never go out.'

4. Stare into the flame and begin to rub your belly in a clockwise direction. Visualise a swirl of fire inside your stomach, filling you with life and passion.

5. As the fire grows, see it rising up your body into your arms. Let your arms rise and begin to sway from side to side until you are at one with the flame. You may wish to stand up to be as tall as a candle flame. Repeat the words of the spell for as long as you feel in the moment.

6. When you feel energised enough to finish the spell, lower your arms and thank the flame for its assistance.

7. Using a douter, put out the candle and light it again whenever you feel your mind clouding over. Focus on the flame until you come back to yourself.

Tip: *Traditional Ayurvedic golden milk is a non-magickal but wonderful way to promote that fire-in-the-belly feeling. In the morning, gently heat 500ml of your choice of milk in a pan on the stove then add 1 tsp of turmeric, ½ tsp of cinnamon, a few slices of fresh ginger, 1 star anise, a dash of black pepper and a splash of honey and bring to a soft simmer for 3–5 minutes. Drink and feel the glorious, nourishing heat of this drink wake up your digestive system without any caffeine.*

Candle magick protection spell

THIS SIMPLE PIECE of candle magick is a quick protection spell to use when you feel like you have just been in contact with someone who drains your energy or you feel like there are people who wish you ill. Deflect their energy and keep your energy vibration high using the practice below.

Perform on the ground to allow the stability of the Earth element to steady you.

You'll need:

+ 1 small black candle

+ 10 tbsp of rock salt

+ 3 tsp of fennel seeds

- 1 crushed clove of garlic

- grapeseed oil

- a small carving implement

- matches/a lighter.

1. On a clean surface, carve your name into the top of the candle.

2. Form the rock salt into a cross shape on the ground.

3. Anoint your candle with the oil, fennel and garlic – using the 'banishing' anointment method (see page 141). As you do this, think clearly about your intention to protect yourself using this spell.

4. Fix the candle in place at the centre of the cross and light it.

5. Repeat these words seven times: 'Flame, protect me. Flame, keep me safe. I am protected; keep all darkness away.'

6. Meditate on the flame for as long as you need, visualising a ball of purple protective energy rising up around you and the spell then settling like a coating on your skin. You may be able to feel this energy resting there. Your own energy is sparkling just below the surface of this protective barrier, shining, safe and sealed in.

7. Allow the candle to burn until it has completely melted then thank the Fire element for helping you in your time of need.

Tip: *You can also use this spell to protect others, including your pets, if you write their name on the candle.*

Self-love fire ritual

THIS CANDLE MAGICK ritual will draw love into your life. This spell is designed not to be used to make a specific person fall in love with you but to welcome the frequency of love into your life in a grounded and wholesome way that will make you feel content in your own skin.

This spell is best performed on a Friday.

You'll need:

+ your usual ritual tools

+ 1 red candle

+ a toothpick or small carving implement

+ 4 rose quartz crystals

+ 1 cup of salt.

For the oil:

- ✦ 4 drops of jasmine essential oil

- ✦ 4 dried red rose petals

- ✦ ½ tsp of cinnamon

- ✦ 1 tsp of orris root powder

- ✦ a small amount of extra-virgin olive oil.

1. Set up and purify your ritual space. Cast your circle and invoke any deities you usually work with.

2. Carve any symbols or sigils into the candle that represent love for you – this could be a heart or a sigil of your own devising.

3. Combine your oil ingredients in a bowl then anoint your candle with the mixture from the top to the middle and then from the bottom to the middle. Place the candle in front of you in the south of the room with four rose quartz crystals around it, then put a small circle of salt around them.

4. Light your candle and look into the flame, saying, 'Venus, set your gaze on me, let rays of love fall on my knee. I am made of burning light; I see myself with true love's sight. In this hour, on this day, let love flow my way.'

5. Visualise waves of love rising up from the heat of the flame and landing on your body. This love

moves in a fluid motion, flowing up from the candle and settling on you from above.

6. Walk in a circle around your sacred space three times, repeating the words. Gather the energy you have created in a ball between your hands, visualising it crackling and buzzing there, then throw it up to the sky. Bring your hands back to your chest to keep some of this light for yourself.

7. Close your sacred space and say thank you to the universe for its help. Light the candle and meditate over it for as long as needed.

Tip: *You can also use this oil to anoint your forehead, heart and Base Chakra before the ritual begins.*

Tip: *You could use a pink candle instead of a red one – which would be softer and gentler – but red holds a much stronger energy.*

Goddess Brigid candle healing ritual

WORKING WITH DEITIES doesn't always have to be a part of your magickal practice but I would recommend it for this particular ritual. Brigid's power can bring light to a dark period where healing is required.

Sacred fire

Any flame used within a ritual setting can be sacred fire but did you know about the origin of the word 'bonfire'? Each year on the Pagan celebration of Samhain (Halloween – traditionally a fire festival), the Ancient Irish peoples would sacrifice and eat the weakest cattle that would be unlikely to survive the long winter ahead. Their bodies would be burned on the ritual Samhain pyres and the skeletons in the flames made them become known as bone fires or *bonfires*. Create your own sacred fire by lighting a candle (tea light, pillar or taper candle – it doesn't make any difference), burning wood in your cauldron or maybe even moving your ritual to the firepit or chiminea outside.

This ritual can be performed inside but I would advocate trying to get outdoors for this powerful ceremony – you might wish to use a fire pit or a bonfire instead of a candle.

You'll need:

✦ 1 white candle

✦ matches/a lighter

✦ white clothing

✦ your usual ritual tools.

1. First thing in the morning, as the sun is just coming up, cast a circle and light a white candle in front of you in a south-facing spot. Invoke the goddess Brigid and ask her to lend her energy to your healing.

2. Explain your situation while looking into the flame. You may wish to have prepared a script beforehand or to read from a journal/diary here, but tell the goddess what it is you want to heal from. Be sure to include anything you are already doing in your life to set this path in motion. For example, if you wanted to heal from panic attacks or experiences of anxiety, explain out loud that you are practising breathing techniques, or have put in place a supportive network of people or

crisis lines that you can speak to to help you calm down. Similarly, if you are healing from a physical ailment, explain that you are regularly trying new healthy ways of being in order to speed up the process of getting back to yourself.

3. Say to the flame:

   'Goddess Brigid [Breed], come to me in my time of need,
   I am ready to serve you and I am ready to heal.
   On this morning, I light a sacred flame,
   I ask you to take my sickness and help it wane.
   Alleviate my [the thing you need help with healing] and help me thrive,
   Help me feel healthy, renewed and alive.
   Brigid, goddess of rebirth, fire and the forge,
   Burn through the old ways and help me transform.'

4. Move around the circle three times in a clockwise motion then come back to stillness in front of the candle.

5. Meditate on the flame for at least five minutes. If you feel Brigid's presence in the circle, note it and say words of thanks.

6. Before you close your circle, show your thanks further by way of a goddess offering. You may wish to recite an appropriate poem, sing a song or

promise to light a white candle for Brigid every day for a month.

7. Snuff out the candle, bid farewell to Brigid and close your circle, ready to ease into your healing journey.

Tip: *When I have performed this ritual in the past, the goddess has appeared to me in a semi-physical form, so be sure to take notice of anything changing in your surroundings as you perform this ritual.*

7

Water

Soothing, cleansing, intuitive

There has never been a time when I haven't felt connected with water.

It is a tonic for the soul that conjures up joy, playfulness and calm.

I have been overjoyed in recent years to hear the science behind cold-water swimming and how, if approached carefully, it can help reset the body as much as breathwork, yoga and meditation.

Water is a feminine element, something that we can sense when she helps us to float, buoying us up to the surface with the translucent and supportive palm of her hand. She is the ruler of emotion, intuition and sensitivity. This is reflected in Tarot, where she is seen in the suit of Cups, the overseer of emotional matters and subjects of the heart.

While Fire is linked to the masculine sun and solar energies, Water is closely entwined with the moon. We might see the moon as a passive sphere in the sky but it is much, much more than a pretty face. The moon is a guiding light in times of trouble and darkness and has a lot of control over our emotional lives. Next time there's a full moon, take note of how you're feeling, sleeping and how many people you've snapped at that day.

As with all the elements, Water has a dark side and there is much lying at the bottom of the seabed that has been lost before its time – the moon, the controller of the tides, must take some of the blame, despite her angelic appearance. Just as these things are gone forever, we can give our troubles to the water so it can take them away on its ever-moving tides. The element of Water is all about the idea of release and letting go so take a deep breath and let the tears take away the pain.

Water correspondences	
Symbol	▽
Direction	West
Zodiac signs	Cancer, Scorpio, Pisces
Alignment	Feminine
Colours	Blue, turquoise, aquamarine
Plants	Burdock, chamomile, catnip, poppies, rose, valerian
Crystals	Aquamarine, lapis lazuli, turquoise, moonstone, amethyst
Humour	Phlegmatic (cold and wet)
Moon phases	New moon
Elementals	Undines, Mermaids
Deities	Tefnut, Poseidon, Neptune, Danu, Damona, Llŷrs
Tarot	Cups
Altar representations	Chalice, bowl of water, cauldron
Time of day	Dusk
Weekday	Monday and Friday
Heavenly bodies	Venus and the Moon
Season	Autumn
Opposing element	Fire

Creating moon water

Moon water can make a wonderful addition to any spell or ritual. Essentially, it is water that has been cleansed and empowered by the light of the full moon.

Moon water can be: drunk throughout the month, used to add potency to magickal workings, used to wash your face or carried around with you in a small vial.

You'll need:

- ✦ a bowl or clear glass bottle

- ✦ as much water as the above will carry – you can use tap, filtered, sea or river water; however, if you are planning to drink the water it's best to make sure it has been cleaned and filtered.

1. On the day of the full moon, pour water into the bowl or bottle and leave it on a windowsill where the moonlight will touch it. Don't worry if it is a cloudy night, the moon's power will still infuse the water.

The power of the moon

As the moon cycles around the Earth, it will turn through different astrological signs. This is something you can use to your advantage – look up what sign the full moon will fall under this month. If the full moon will be in Aries, use the moon water to drive your plans forward; if it is in Cancer, you can use your moon water in any rituals that are focussed on emotions and letting go.

As well as moon water, we can also empower and cleanse our crystals on the full moon. Leave them out on your windowsill every full moon to charge them up and make their energies shine.

2. In the morning, thank the moon for blessing your water and store the liquid in a safe container, such as a glass bottle or jar. It will remain potent throughout the month.

Herbs and plants associated with the Water element

Softness and delicate flavours characterise herbs and plants ruled over by Water. Think of them as a gentle nudge back to wellness and a hug before bed.

Rose (*Rosa*)

IS THERE ANYTHING more gorgeous than rose? Its fragrance and scent are entrancing and seductive, something reflected in its long history of being used in love magick.

But rose's qualities don't always invoke the saucier side of life. Rose is a calming presence that helps us sink into our Water-governed feminine energy, enhancing our intuition and engaging with our womb space or inner femininity.

Connecting with these aspects of self can be so important as we begin to heal from a masculine-dominated society. Rose buds are also something I put into my tea when I know I need to be treating myself better. It is my opinion that a cup of rose tea is the first step to self-care and self-love.

Magickal properties: anti-anxiety, self-love, friendship, calmness, inner and outer beauty, feminine intuition, sexuality

Raspberry leaf (*Rubus idaeus*)

THIS ONE IS traditionally used to help with menstrual issues and is often called 'the women's herb' as it aided with childbirth, cramps and fertility. However, raspberry leaf is beneficial to all as it is known to soothe the adrenal glands, where we produce cortisol, helping us to release super-sensitive stress responses that might put us into fight-or-flight mode.

It works well in teas as well as ritual baths to enhance femininity but also relaxes us and helps us sleep. If you experience pre-menstrual tension that often exacerbates mood swings and symptoms of overwhelm, then raspberry tea is one to drink regularly but especially around your period.

Magickal properties: femininity, hormone balance, calm, de-stressing, menstrual pain, sleep

Oat straw (*Avena sativa*)

OH, OAT STRAW; you have calmed my nerves and brought me back to myself so many times. Dried oat straw is sweeter than you think it is going to taste and has a soothing effect on the body and mind. If you are experiencing physical symptoms of stress, burnout and fatigue then oat straw in a tea or infusion can alleviate these by helping to calm the nervous system and giving you a restful sleep.

Thanks to its Water-ruled tendencies, it's also a good one for helping with kidney and urinary issues, which can often flare up in times of intense pressure.

Magickal properties: calm, soothing, sleep, anti-anxiety

Ritual bathing and cleansing

Dim the lights and get the music on: it's bath time. If you've never experienced a ritual bath, you are in for a treat. When I have practised ritual bathing, it has primarily been for cleansing my body to prepare myself for performing a long ritual or magickal working that requires a lot of concentration or components. The bath water allows the physical detritus of the day to fall away. However, it has the purpose of calming the body and lowering our heart rate but also helping us slip into that slightly dreamlike state that is so commonly assumed in ritual work. Through half-closed eyes and the dim steamy light under our lashes, the world seems to shift, and the lights and messages of other worlds might begin to slip through. By helping us after our mental and spiritual state, ritual bathing cleanses not only our physical bodies but also our mind and spirit and is a pure joy to perform.

How to prepare a ritual bath

HERE IS AN example of a common ritual bath designed to purify and cleanse you before magickal working.

You'll need:

+ around 300g of Epsom salts

+ a few sprigs of rosemary

+ 8 drops of frankincense oil

+ 8 drops of lavender oil

+ 6 drops of cedar oil

+ 10 dried rosebuds or rose petals

+ 2 white candles

+ selenite

+ clear quartz

- a bundle of sage or your chosen method of cleansing a room

- a speaker or music device

- matches/a lighter.

1. Set up your bathroom in a way to minimise distractions – move the cat's litter tray, the shampoo bottles and the toothpaste so that the bath and the space around it are clear from debris.

2. Cleanse the room with sage or with sound vibrations.

3. You may wish to play music, so put your playlist on, but once you have started creating your ritual bath it's important to leave technology behind and move your device away from the bath. It might be tempting to skip to the next track, but this is an added distraction and can detract from your cleansing intention.

4. Next, begin to run the water and add the salts. Quietly stir these in with your hand, first three times clockwise (deosil) then three times anti-clockwise (widdershins) to bring in balance, consciously thinking about your intention as you do so. Say, 'This water cleanses and purifies me,' bringing that intention to the forefront of your thoughts.

5. Then add the oils and herbs, giving thanks for their presence as you place them in the water, always keeping your intention in mind.

6. Once the bath is run, add your clear quartz and selenite around the edge (not in the water) and light the white candles.

7. Slip into the bath and begin to meditate on your intention. Visualise the water lapping at your skin and making you pure. You may wish to imagine the water glowing with a white light over your body. Try to keep your thoughts focussed on purification and the ritual work you are about to perform. If your mind wanders, bring it back to your purpose using the breath.

8. Stay in the bath for as long as you need. The absolute bare minimum of time to spend there is 20 minutes, as this allows the salts to begin cleansing your body on a physical level, but, if you can, I would recommend spending an hour there if not longer.

9. As you are about to leave the bath, thank the water and its contents for cleansing you. You may then begin your further magickal workings.

Tip: *Ritual bathing is a wonderful thing to do but is not always possible to perform before every ritual and you may not have access to a bath. A quicker alternative is to hang bundles of herbs in your shower, allowing the steam to release their properties as you wash your body. You can also put dried herbs into a tea infuser and hang that in your shower!*

Ritual bath for protection

YOU MAY WISH to make a bath into a ritual in and of itself. The bath below creates a protective layer around your body and can be performed at any time you feel you need magickal help to keep your spiritual or mental barriers in place.

You'll need:

+ around 300g of Epsom salts

+ 2–3 cinnamon sticks

+ a small bunch of mugwort

+ 8 drops of lavender oil

+ 6 drops of wild orange oil

- ✦ 8 drops of cedar oil

- ✦ 6 drops of sandalwood oil (optional)

- ✦ 2 black candles

- ✦ smoky quartz

- ✦ amethyst

- ✦ a bundle of sage or your chosen method of cleansing a room

- ✦ a speaker or music device

- ✦ matches/a lighter.

1. Set up your bath as in the cleansing ritual above, setting your intention of protection.

2. Once you are in your bath, visualise a glowing purple force field around your body. This energy is a barrier between your energy centres and any unwanted external influence. Repeat 'I am protected' as a mantra while you are in the bath.

3. Drain the water and thank the components of the bath for helping you today.

Guided meditation for letting go of anxiety

Over the centuries, so many ships have been lost at sea. Years later when they are hauled to the surface, the ships need constant immersion in water for them to keep their shape – without water they disintegrate and fragment. The feminine force of the ocean has claimed these vessels as her own; they will forever be a part of the water now.

We can harness this same power by speaking to the Water element through guided meditation. By giving our worries to the Water, she takes them as her own – they can never be ours again.

Perform this meditation lying down on the night of the full moon. It might be a good idea to do this undisturbed in the bath or straight after a shower, feeling the calm of the Water element around you. You can also download a recording of this meditation from jenniferlanewrites.com/meditations.

1. *Slowly get yourself into a peaceful, meditative state. Your eyes are closed or your gaze can be soft and unfocussed. Your mind is clear and your body feels light as if you are surrounded by water.*

2. *Begin by visualising yourself floating in a still pool of water. Your limbs are spread out like a star and*

you feel calm as the water holds you up. Tall rocks are around you, surrounding and protecting you. What is the scene around you like? Are you in a rainforest surrounded by dense vegetation and the soft sounds of birds of paradise? Or are you in a pool closer to home with a gentle waterfall cascading over rocks? Remember, this is your pool now and you can return here at any time you feel like you need to be held.

3. *In your pool, your eyes start to focus on a small opening in the rocks up ahead and you find your body floating towards it. You slip effortlessly between the rocks and you find yourself now in a slow-moving river filled with lily pads. You feel serene, watching the ducks swim in and out of the lily pads and beautiful songbirds fly overhead.*

4. *Up in front of you is an especially large green lily pad and the water deposits you on it so that you are sitting in its centre. It feels so lovely to be held up by the water and the lily pad, floating along with the current.*

5. *You look to your left and see a turn in the river. After the turn, the water gets choppier and, in the distance, you can see a whirlpool. But don't worry, you are safe. The lily pad you are travelling on is stopped in its tracks as it softly comes into contact with a host of other lilies growing in the water. You are surrounded*

by calm and stillness while the whirlpool continues to swirl up ahead.

6. *Now is the time to think about the anxieties you would like to let go of. Take a moment to do this.*

7. *Lie down on the plant's green body and allow your fingers to trail in the water over the edges. Bring to mind the issues that are worrying you right now. Imagine their crackly energy travelling down from your Third Eye, the space between your eyebrows, and into your neck, then your shoulders and into your arms. They make their way through your fingertips and into the water around you. As they touch its surface, the area is darkened with their negativity.*

8. *Visualise this darkness seeping into the water current and being taken into the whirlpool ahead. See the energy swirling around and around, going further down and down. The whirlpool makes a loud crashing noise as it swallows your anxieties one by one, leaving no trace in the clear, crystalline waters.*

9. *Stay here on your lily pad for as long as you need, releasing worry and feeling it borne away and transformed by the healing water below.*

10. *Once you have finished, take a big deep releasing breath. The lily pad begins to move again, now that you feel lighter and more carefree. But it doesn't*

carry you forward; it heads towards a hidden watercourse to your left. You gently slip through the rocks on your lily pad and find yourself back in the calm pool where you started. You feel fresh, happy and much more relaxed.

11. *Take another deep breath through your nose into your belly and, as you exhale, luxuriate in the beautiful waters of this secret place.*

12. *Open your eyes and remember that feeling of lightness throughout the rest of your day.*

Water goddesses and gods

Tefnut is the Ancient Egyptian goddess of rain, moisture and dew and was often worshipped to keep the rains coming down to replenish the River Nile – water, of course, would have been incredibly important to this desert civilisation. She is depicted as a woman with a lioness's head and a solar disk headdress flanked by two cobras. Cobras were seen as protective symbols and Tefnut was the protector of several gods. As a goddess with a strong connection to Water, commune with her when you want to let an emotion or a current situation wash away from your life – or if you are in need of protection.

Water elementals

Perhaps the least-known elemental is the undine. This Water spirit is often depicted as a beautiful woman lounging on the rocks with her toes dipped in the water, making her akin to the mermaid but without the fishy tail. Secretive and quiet, this maiden of the Water element embodies traditionally feminine qualities and is the keeper of emotion, intuition and compassion.

'Unda' is the Latin for wave, which is exactly where you'll find the undines. They can be seen inhabiting any natural space with water, such as the sea, rivers, lakes and waterfalls. While she may be soft and sensual, the undine is not afraid to unleash the power of the waves when she senses that emotions are being trodden over by the dominant forces. In this way, I see the undine as sticking up for the underdog and those who are not afraid to show their true selves and feelings in a masculine-centric world.

Show your respect for the Water elementals when you:

+ spend time in water and luxuriate in ritual baths or showers

+ verbalise your emotions

+ add turquoise, angel agate and other watery stones to your home and outdoor space

+ make fluid movements and mindfully flow within
  your body.

Water is such a deliciously healing element and, once you
have earned its attention, the undines can bring you introspection, depth of emotion and a new level of kindness.

Honouring the Water element

Simple ways to show your appreciation include:

+ spending time walking by bodies of water and
  saying words of thanks

+ wild swimming

+ making a small wildlife pond in your garden

+ creating a small water feature

+ decorating your home or workspace with pictures
  of water (I have a print of *Hylas and the Nymphs* by
  John William Waterhouse on my fridge)

+ viewing a livestream of the tides going in and out
  online

+ making moon water (and carrying it with you in a
  small jar or vial)

- wearing blue, turquoise or aquamarine

- looking for the water placements in your astrological chart

- having a tank for aquatic plants in your home (if you want to push the boat out!).

Creating a Water altar

- Incorporate a chalice or bowl filled with salt water or moon water

- add Tarot cards from the suit of Cups

- place shells or stones made smooth by a river or the sea

- face the altar in a westward direction.

Water rituals and spells

The magick below taps into the healing power of water, reconnecting us with our selves, our sensuality and our emotions. It is so common for the Water element (as well as the Earth element) to be ignored due to its associations with femininity and slower practices in a world that wants to drain every ounce of productivity out of us.

But take the time now to sink into the water and let these rituals soothe your soul.

Water ritual to bring balance

THERE ARE TIMES in our lives when stress takes over. It could be a steady build-up or a sudden deluge. I've had both happen to me but the feeling is the same – complete overwhelm, outbursts of panic, insomnia and total dread of how much is still left to do. In the working world where deadlines often mount up, this feeling might be very familiar but it also might exist in a messy house, with a friend who keeps putting the pressure on or with a certain family member who refuses to see your point of view.

Water is a great balancer. Not only do water's energetics soothe and console, but its physical properties also remind us of equilibrium; still water is always level thanks to gravity and when shaken will always look to return to its flat neutral state.

This ritual harnesses the element of Water to return us to a balanced state of being where stress and upsets can leave us freely, flowing away like a stream. This ritual can be performed inside or can be adapted to incorporate a flowing water source outside.

You'll need:

+ a bowl of water (large enough to fit both hands in at once)

+ 1 white candle

+ 1 black candle

+ your usual ritual items.

1. Cast your circle, spending extra time visualising the element of Water flowing around you.

2. Light the candles in front of you – black on the left and white on the right – in a westerly direction and set the bowl of water between the two.

3. Close your eyes and say three times:

> 'Water, bring balance.
> Water, make me whole.
> Negativity, ebb away.
> Positivity, in flow.'

4. When you have done this, plunge your hands into the water and hold them there.

5. Visualise negative energy flowing out of your left hand into the water. You might see this energy as dark, dense or cloudy, coming up from your feet and through your whole body, down your

left arm. As it hits the water, strongly visualise the water neutralising this energy, removing its negativity entirely.

6. Next, visualise bright, sparkling, positive energy rising from the water and into your right hand, rising like a wave through your entire body.

7. Continue with this visualisation so that negative energy continuously leaves your body and is replaced by positive energy, until there is no dense energy left inside you. Do this for as long as you need.

8. Thank the Water element profusely then blow out your candles and say, 'So mote it be.'

9. Close your circle as normal and use the water from the bowl to water your plants or leave it as a bird bath or hedgehog drinking spot outside.

Tip: *After step 7, you might wish to dance in your circle and let the new positive energy settle in your body by making fluid motions. No one can see you, so feel free to dance as water moves, ebbing and flowing, twisting and falling. Have some music handy in case the urge takes you and dance for as long as you wish.*

Water energy spell to soothe anxiety

THIS SPELL JAR is small and compact and can be carried with you whenever you need to soothe yourself. Pop it in your pocket the night before a big meeting or have it in your bag when meeting a large group of people.

You'll need:

+ 1 small glass vial

+ 1 white candle

+ small chips of rose quartz (or you could use 1 tsp of Himalayan salt)

+ 2 tsp of dried oat straw

+ 2 tsp of dried chamomile flowers

+ 4 whole dried rosebuds

+ a bowl of salt water

+ matches/a lighter

+ optional: 1 tsp of powdered liquorice root.

1. First, immerse the vial into the bowl of salt water to cleanse it. Thoroughly dry the vial before use.

2. Insert the rose quartz chips or salt into the bottom of the vial then add the Water-ruled herbs on top. As you are doing this, visualise your intention coming to fruition, saying, 'I am calm; I am no longer anxious.'

3. See this sense of calm in your mind's eye and picture where it sits in your body. Visualise a white light spreading across your chest and up into your temples.

4. Once the vial is filled to the brim, light the white candle and allow its wax to melt. Drip the wax into the opening of the vial and insert the cork or stopper. Continue to drip the wax around the stopper and on top of it so it is completely sealed by the wax.

5. Hold it in your hand and say a few final words to solidify your intent.

6. Allow to cool and keep the spell jar with you about your person.

Tip: *At times when you might experience anxiety, hold the spell jar in your hand and feel it over with your thumb. For this reason, you might like to carve symbols or sigils of relaxation and calm into the wax or the cork stopper so that you can feel these with your hand.*

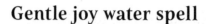

Gentle joy water spell

THE WORD 'RESILIENCE' is banded about a lot in modern life. To be successful in a conventional workplace, you need to be resilient, have thick skin and just be tough. Personally, I have never found this language to be helpful – it's about as archaic as the phrase 'man up'.

Many of us are soft-skinned and sensitive to strong emotions so that intense blasts of any feeling – whether it is positive or negative – can leave us reeling for days and become overwhelming. As someone who fits firmly into the sensitive category, I know just how strong certain emotions can feel in the body.

That's why this spell is designed to provide gentle waves of happiness and contentment instead.

You'll need:

+ a cup of hot water

+ a sprinkle of dried chamomile flowers

+ a sprinkle of dried violets

+ 4 white candles

+ a large bowl

+ matches/a lighter.

1. On or near your altar, light the candles at each point of the compass.

2. Steep the flowers in the hot water and leave to cool for 20 minutes on your altar, with the cup in the middle of the candles.

3. Once infused, pour the water into the large bowl and scoop some up in your hands.

4. Look down into the water between your palms, watching how the nearby candles create light on its surface. As they shift and flicker in the water, notice how your hands are filled with gentleness, brightness and the nourishing beauty of the Water element.

5. Say to the water, 'Water bring me softness, Water make me smile; Water bring me joy – contentment is mine.'

6. Gently bring your hands to your face over the bowl and wash your face and neck in this sweet-smelling water.

7. Use the water on your plants the next time they need it.

Tip: *Perform this simple spell at the start of any self-care routine.*

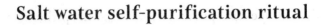

Salt water self-purification ritual

THE DEBRIS OF the modern world can often settle on our minds and bodies, making us feel heavy, swamped and confused. This ritual is designed to help clear the energetic clutter and bring back our own unique energies. While not entirely necessary, you may wish to perform this ritual 'skyclad' (the witchy term for naked!) for an extra layer of purification. If you prefer to be clothed then wear white clothing.

You'll need:

+ 1 white candle

+ sandalwood incense

+ half a cup of sea salt

+ a small bowl of water

+ a towel

+ matches/a lighter

+ your usual ritual tools.

1. Cast a circle, invoke the Goddess and meditate inside the sacred space for 5 minutes, thinking about your ritual intention of self-purification.

2. Light a candle and state your intention to be

cleansed of the outside world and to return to your own energy.

3. Take several pinches of salt and drop them into the water bowl, mixing the two together in a clockwise motion.

4. Slowly and mindfully, rub the salt water into your skin, starting with your feet and ending with your face. As you do this, repeat, 'Goddess cleanse me, I am purified. Goddess cleanse me, I am purified.' You may wish to stand on a towel as you do this.

5. This is a meditative practice so take as long as you need and you can always visualise negative energy leaving your body as you go, fading into the earth below you. How do you feel now? How does this purified energy sit in and around your body? Take note of any peacefulness and lightness you may be feeling.

6. When you are finished, thank the Goddess for her help today and close your circle. Keep the salt water on your skin or shower it off.

Tip: *You may wish to steam your face with chamomile water afterwards and apply liberal amounts of moisturiser to keep your glowing, cleansed energy sealed in.*

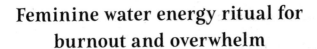

Feminine water energy ritual for burnout and overwhelm

AS THE RULER of emotion, Water can provide great nourishment when we are feeling completely depleted or emotionally at the end of our tether. The final ritual in this book uses bathing to help release the symptoms of burnout, nourish your soul and calm your body at the deepest level.

Follow the advice for ritual bathing on page 178 to get the most out of this practice.

You'll need:

+ around 300g of Epsom salts

+ fresh lemon balm leaves

+ 8 drops of lavender oil

+ 10 dried rosebuds or rose petals

+ a large pinch of skullcap

+ a selection of pink and white candles

+ rose quartz

+ moonstone

+ a bundle of sage or your chosen method of cleansing a room

+ a speaker or music device

+ matches/a lighter

+ optional: 6 drops of holy basil oil.

1. Set up your bathroom the way you want it and cleanse the space.

2. Add the salts to the running water. Stir these in with your hand anti-clockwise (widdershins) with the intent of reducing stress and creating a soft calm. Repeat 'This water soothes and heals me' nine times, bringing that intention to the forefront of your thoughts.

3. Next, mindfully pour in the oils and herbs, keeping your intention in mind.

4. Add the crystals to the sides of the bath and light the candles when the bath is run.

5. Slip into the bath and begin to meditate on your intention, visualising the water around you healing and repairing your body and brain. Whisper the words 'Water make me whole, Water heal me' as you do so.

6. Making your eyelids soft, look at the water from under your lashes and picture a soft pink light bathing your skin and everything around you. You are surrounded by femininity that will penetrate your body. You may also wish to bring the rose quartz to your Third Eye.

7. Stay in the bath for as long as you need, absorbing this feminine energy.

8. As you are about to leave the bath, thank the water and its contents for cleansing you.

Closing

I hope you have enjoyed this journey through the world of witchcraft and discovering how we can tap into the power of the elements to bring joy, healing and contentment into our lives.

We might live in a fast-paced, ever-turning world but there are so many of us now who are expressing our love of a slower pace of life. We don't want photocopiers, strip lights and concrete; we want bonfires, barefoot walks and waking up with the rising sun.

I have found that a world with its eyes open to magick is a happier place. Since my own spiritual awakening back in 2018, I have been slowly shedding my darkness.

Those hollow places of stress, insomnia and turmoil I once inhabited have been wafted from my chest like black smoke coiling its way out of an open window. What has been left in its place is a new strength and a sense of 'I can' that I didn't think was possible at the start of my journey. Reading back over that statement, it might seem blasé or gushy, but for someone who had been struggling with the devastating effects of anxiety and depression for fifteen years before my learning began, I am truly amazed at the power this path has had. I know that it is completely and entirely possible to reconnect with yourself and the world around you after experiencing the lowest point in your life. Five years ago, I didn't think I could continue. There were days I didn't get out of bed. There were days I didn't even open the blinds to catch a glimpse of the sky. My reconnection with the land and the elements came slowly over several weeks and months. Tentative walks. Eyes closed. Chin held up to the sun. And, slowly, things started to get better.

Witchcraft has given me so much – not only do I know that I can rely on the supportive net of magick in times of need, I feel more spiritually connected with the seasons, currents and the more-than-human world than I ever have been before. If, at any point in time, I find myself feeling low, frazzled or disconnected, I can open my front door and find myself in a green space in virtually no time at all – no matter where I am in the world.

This path is open and available to you too. All it takes is a quiet afternoon, a slow deep breath and the gentle rustle of leaves to get started.

For those living in more urban areas, green places might be slightly further away, but cultivating herbs and wildlife-friendly plants on our windowsills and balconies can provide instant access to the delicately veined patterns of nature. Open your window – let in the air, wind and fire! Let them cleanse you, soothe you and re-energise you.

Before I go, I want to share some observations with you that you might have already come across yourself in your own journey but I think they are important to talk about. There are people in this world who are still living in the old world order – the one that is dominated by masculine energy, violence and brute force. These people might not be aware of their mindsets and the damaging social myths they perpetuate. However, something I have noticed over the past few years – and something I've been watching closely – is that the world seems to be shifting. You might have noticed powerful bursts of energy, community spirit and lively debate as people open themselves up to a world that is not constrained by old ways of thinking.

We are slowly entering a space of balance, where people can choose their own energy – whether it is masculine, feminine or somewhere in between – and patterns of living without being forced to adhere to the old negative cycles of past ages. In most corners of the world, magick is no longer something to be feared and 'wicked' women are not pawns to be hung at the gallows to set an example. Many of us are returning to softer, gentler ways of being and trying to figure out how we can still live calm, centred and joyful lives under the current capitalist structures. We rejoice in the vibrant colours of nature, we honour our emotions and we move mindfully to savour the smell of rain and the feel of grass between our toes.

People are waking up and – if you are reading this – you have too.

I have hope for a witchier world that reveres the beauty of nature and I firmly believe that we are entering a new age. The more of us stopping to remember what it feels like to live at one with the innate energies of the world, the happier, healthier and more whole we can become.

I wish you the very best of luck on your own journey to healing and empowerment. May this book be a supportive guide for you as you navigate your journey back to wellness and wholeness. Living a connected, rooted life is entirely possible and it is within our reach.

I'll leave you with one final blessing of healing that you can repeat to yourself each morning or use as a charm for your favourite piece of jewellery or a crystal that you will carry with you. Say these words in the shower, and in times when you need them the

most and feel the power of the elements gather close to
your skin:

> 'Earth, Air, Fire, Water,
> Ground me, inspire me,
> Impassion and soothe me.
> All four elements, by my side,
> Bring your healing and be my guides.'

A very witchy appendix

In this appendix, you'll find a compendium of essential magickal associations within witchcraft. Understanding these basics is vital to being able to perform the spells and rituals in this book with the most effect.

Helpful guides to magickal correspondences

Days of the week

Sunday: Literally, the sun's day – great for magic involving personal victories, wealth and success. It is a powerful, confident day.

Monday: The moon's day is dedicated to women's mysteries, psychic abilities, emotions and femininity. Turn your face up to her light as if she was the sun and absorb all her softness.

Tuesday: The day of Mars. The Roman god of war allows you to summon extra strength and courage today, especially when dealing with conflict. Stick by your guns and don't say sorry for something that wasn't your fault.

Wednesday: Ruled by Mercury, Wednesday is a day for communication. Spells and rituals around clarity and finding answers are useful here. You might also want to test your public speaking skills, memory or intelligence today.

Thursday: Belonging to Jupiter, Thursday is here to bring wealth, abundance, confidence, strength and good health. Jupiter is a commanding presence, often referred to in mythology as 'the king of the gods'. Today is a day for holding your head high.

Friday: It's Friday, I'm in love – and quite rightly so. Friday is the day of Venus, so it is good for working with issues of romance, fertility and self-love. Be kind and soft with yourself on a Friday.

Saturday: The serious nature of Saturn ruling over this day means that protection, focussing, self-discipline and banishing magick will be especially potent.

Herbs and plants for general use

These twelve herbs are some of the most commonly used within a magickal practice so it is best to stock up on these and have either a dried or fresh supply available to you.

Basil: money, good luck, love, purification

Bay: prosperity, manifestation, psychic dreams, purification

Chamomile: promotes sleep, reduces anxiety, calms the body and the mind

Garden sage: purification, repelling negativity, attracting positivity, wisdom, gaining knowledge

Lavender: reducing anxiety, promoting peace and love, protection, sleep, purification/cleansing, wellbeing

Lemon balm: healing, joy, easing heartache

Mint: prosperity, abundance, love, protection, health, inspiring action, energising the body and mind, wellbeing

Mugwort: enhancing psychic ability, lucid dreaming,

Rose: friendship, self-love, romantic love, gentle healing

Rosemary: psychic and spiritual protection, happiness, easing depression

Thyme: loyalty, good health, restful sleep, courage

Yarrow: divination, foresight

Crystals

Whether you are just starting out or looking to expand your collection, these crystals are the most useful ones to have at home to help with healing. Always make sure to source these from an ethical dealer (see page 219 for my list of ethical suppliers).

Amethyst: I use amethyst for protection and balance. Have this crystal around you to keep psychic vampires at bay while also calming your nerves and coming back into line with yourself

Aventurine: an excellent stone for physical and mental health, particularly around preventing stress. It is a very calming and soothing crystal that protects your energy field

Carnelian: confidence, happiness, self-esteem, inspiration and courage. I carry this whenever I need a boost

Citrine: learning, creativity, new beginnings and focus. It's also a good stone to have around if your worries stem from money

Clear quartz: clarity, clear-headedness and releasing negativity; it is also a useful stand-in for other crystals if you do not have them at hand as it channels all different kinds of energy when imbued with intent

Malachite: eases depression and boosts the immune system. This is a crystal that helps to regulate mood swings and bring emotional stability

Rose quartz: a stone for matters of the heart. Calms emotions, enhances feminine energy and brings harmony to romantic and platonic relationships

Selenite: this is a self-cleansing stone; use it to cleanse objects and areas. This is a crystal associated with the moon (Selene) and can be helpful with menstrual issues or when used in moon rituals

Smoky quartz: protection, grounding and releasing negativity. I keep some by my bed to keep away negative energy while I'm in a lucid dreaming state

Turquoise: a stone ruled over by the throat and communication, this is a good one for speaking your truth, meditation and mental clarity. It supports emotional stability and inspires beauty in your life

Colours

Colour comes into almost every spell, ritual or charm – take good note of these colour correspondences to make your magick as potent as possible.

Black: ward/absorb negativity, remove hexes, physical and psychic protection, contacting Spirit

Blue (dark): the Water element, truth, protection, change, meditation, health, wellbeing, harmony, truth, inner peace

Blue (light): peace, patience, truth, wisdom, happiness, protection, psychic awareness, intuition, new opportunities, understanding, tranquillity

Brown: the Earth element, the home and hearth, endurance, groundedness, stability, animal healing, concentration

Gold: power, prosperity, money magick, success, solar magick

Green: the Earth element, abundance, prosperity, wealth, the working world, renewal, growth, fertility, mental and physical health, luck

Grey: Meditation, neutralising negativity, astral travel, complex issues

Orange: energy, stimulation, attraction, vitality, adaptability to sudden changes, encouragement, power, intellect

Pink: friendship, love, romance, compassion, calm

Purple: spiritual communication, psychic development, intuition, luxury, protection, the occult, meditation

Red: the Fire element, passion, physical love/ sexuality, intensity, physical needs, strength, energy and the body, health (specifically virility), bravery and outward confidence, willpower, magnetism

Silver: the moon, meditation, psychic development, success, balance, wards negativity, memory

White: purification, protection, enlightenment, truth, meditation, peace, sincerity, cleansing, clarity, understanding

Yellow: The Air element, happiness, joy, mental intelligence, mental clarity, knowledge, exams/ studying, inspiration, imagination, communication, self-confidence, sense of self

Further reading

Witchcraft

Hedge Witch: A Guide to Solitary Witchcraft by Rae Beth

Witchery: Embrace the Witch Within by Juliet Diaz

The Witch of the Woods: Spells, Charms, Divinations, Remedies and Folklore by Kiley Mann

Natural Magic by Doreen Valiente

Folk Witchcraft: A Guide to Lore, Land, and the Familiar Spirit for the Solitary Practitioner by Roger J. Horne

Sacred Earth Celebrations by Glennie Kindred

Wild Magic: Celtic Folk Traditions for the Solitary Practitioner by Danu Forest

Herblore and herbal uses

Witch's Garden by Sandra Lawrence

Culpeper's Complete Herbal by Nicholas Culpeper

Green Witchcraft: Folk Magic, Fairy Lore & Herb Craft by Ann Moura

Earth Magic by Lindsay Squires

Seasonal living and connection with nature

Braiding Sweetgrass by Robin Wall Kimmerer

Losing Eden: Why Our Minds Need the Wild by Lucy Jones

Silent Earth: Averting the Insect Apocalypse by Dave Goulson

Thin Places by Kerri ní Dochartaigh

The Living Mountain by Nan Shepherd

Tiffany Francis newsletters – tiffanyfrancisbaker.com/

Creative Countryside newsletters – creativecountryside.com/

Other elemental practices

Between Heaven and Earth – A Guide to Chinese Medicine by Harriet Beinfield and Efrem Korngold

Nourishing Destiny: The Inner Tradition of Chinese Medicine by Lonny S. Jarrett

Ethical stores to buy your magickal tools

T he witchcraft community has a duty of care to the world and must protect it at all costs – selecting our tools and ingredients from ethical sources helps to minimise environmental and social impact and promote healthier practices. These are stores I have used to source my own magickal tools or which come highly recommended. All have an online presence that accept orders but I have included the location of those with physical stores.

UK

Cosmic Order, Greater Manchester – cosmic-order-ltd.
  sumupstore.com
Crooked Books, West Yorkshire – crookedbooks.co.uk
She's Lost Control, London – sheslostcontrol.co.uk
Luna Amatores, Carlisle – lunaamatores.co.uk
Spooks, Haworth, West Yorkshire – spooks.co.uk
Watkins Books, London – watkinsbooks.com
Treadwell's, London – treadwells-london.com

The Atlantis Bookshop, London – theatlantisbookshop.
com
Global Tribe, Leeds – globalcrystals.com
Crystal Auras – crystalauras.co.uk
crystal + the moon – crystalandthemoon.com

North America

Natural Collective LLC, Illinois – naturalcollectivellc.
com
Beyond Bohemian, Florida – beyondbohemian.com
The Spirit Nectar, Montana – etsy.com/shop/
TheSpiritnectar
Ravenstone, Massachusetts – ravenstonegifts.com
Rite of Ritual, Alberta – riteofritual.com
White Magick Alchemy – whitemagickalchemy.com

Australasia

Ethical Crystals Sunshine Coast – ethicalcrystalssun-
shinecoast.com
Hand in Hand, Yeppoon, Queensland, Australia – hand-
inhandyeppoon.com.au
Serenity Crystals, Wellington, New Zealand – serenity-
crystals.co.nz

Glossary

anointing – the process of ceremonially dressing a candle with oil

amulet – a small item or piece of jewellery that repels negative energies from the wearer

athame – a ceremonial dagger used in rituals or on a witch's altar as a symbol of masculinity

boline – traditionally, a white-handled knife used to cut herbs, and held on a witch's altar

book of shadows – a diary or journal used to record personal spells, rituals, potions and other magickal workings

cardinal sign – the zodiac sign that starts a season, namely Aries (spring), Cancer (summer), Libra (autumn) and Capricorn (winter)

Celtic Ogham – an early Irish alphabet system named after the Celtic god of eloquence and literacy

chalice – a ceremonial cup used to represent the feminine divine on a witch's altar

charm – focussing a magick spell on a specific object, which is then carried about the person or hung about the house (amulets and talismans are forms of charms)

circle – a sacred space in which to contain and work with magick douter – a candle snuffer, usually made of metal

green witch – a witch with close links to nature magick, herbs and plants

magic/magick – a spiritual force that can be used to enhance, influence or change the way something happens

Pagan/Paganism – someone who celebrates the beauty of nature, observes the seasons' cycles and sees nature as innately spiritual (not the same as a witch, see below)

pentacle – a five-pointed star

pentagram – an encircled five-pointed star

ritual – a ceremonial focussing of magickal energies to reach an intended outcome

rune – a letter from a Germanic alphabet system that is often used as magickal symbols

scry – divining the future, usually by consulting objects such as a crystal ball, a black mirror (traditionally a reflective dark surface like obsidian), a candle flame or a bowl of water

sigil – a symbol or sign imbued with magickal intent

spell – a focussing of magickal energies to produce the intended outcome

talisman – a small item or piece of jewellery that attracts power and other qualities to the wearer

Wheel of the Year – a circular depiction of the eight Pagan festivals – Samhain, Yule, Imbolc, Ostara, Beltane, Litha, Lammas and Mabon – showing how everything is cyclical

Wicca – a denomination of witchcraft that uses positive
magick and often performs elaborate ceremonies and
rituals as part of its practice

witch – someone who uses magick and charges objects
with energy to bring about change

CReferences

1 https://www.rcpsych.ac.uk/mental-health/problems-disorders/seasonal-affective-disorder-(sad).

2 Gazzaniga, M. S., and Heatherton, T. F. (2003). *Psychological Science: Mind, Brain, and Behavior.* New York, NY: W. W. Norton, p. 336.

3 https://www.hse.gov.uk/statistics/causdis/stress.pdf.

4 Breit, S., Kupferberg, A., Rogler, G., & Hasler, G. (2018). Vagus Nerve as Modulator of the Brain–Gut Axis in Psychiatric and Inflammatory Disorders. *Frontiers in Psychiatry, 9.* https://doi.org/10.3389/fpsyt.2018.00044.

Acknowledgements

I couldn't end this book without thanking the readers of *The Wheel: A Witch's Path to Healing Through Nature*. So many of you reached out looking for a practical guide on navigating the pressures of the modern world as a witch. Thank you for all your heartfelt, beautiful messages: I hope you have found what you are looking for in this book.

I also want to say a huge thank you to Hannah, Charlotte and Rach at September Publishing for giving me the chance to write *The Witch's Survival Guide*. It has been an absolute pleasure to work with you again and keep talking about a subject so close to my heart.

Charlotte Atyeo at Greyhound Literary – you are a superstar. Thank you to Will, Joss, Claire, Em, Carly, Nic and my family for all your support and encouragement. And how could I not say thank you to my best pal, Linnet, for keeping me company and purring in my ear while I wrote this book curled up by the fire? What a little angel you are.

About the author

Jennifer Lane is a green witch and nature writer with a background in wildlife communications. Her first book, *The Wheel: A Witch's Path to Healing Through Nature*, came out in 2021. As a journalist she has written for *Vogue*, the *Guardian* and the BBC, promoting the wider health benefits of nature, birdwatching and living in tune with the land. In 2018, she won a Northern Writers' Award, and her first YA novel will be released in September 2023. Jennifer is based near Manchester with her partner and a calico cat called Linnet.

Get in touch

Instagram and TikTok: @thegreenwitchwriter

Twitter: @jennlanewrites

Or contact me through my website and sign up to my newsletter: jenniferlanewrites.com